Easy Money For Lazy People

Recognize Opportunities

Take Action

Start a Business Online

and Make Money

Luke F. Gregory © 2016

Legal Disclaimer

Copyright © 2016 Luke F. Gregory. All rights reserved worldwide.

No part of this material may be used, reproduced, distributed or transmitted in any form and by any means whatsoever, including without limitation photocopying, recording or other electronic or mechanical methods or by any information storage and retrieval system, without the prior written permission of the author, except for brief excerpts in a review.

This book is intended to provide general information only. Neither the author nor publisher offers any legal or other professional advice. If you need professional advice, you should seek advice from the appropriate licensed professional. This book does not provide complete information on the subject matter covered. This book is not intended to address specific requirements, either for an individual or an organization. This book aims to be used only as a general guide, and not as a sole source of information on the subject matter. While the author has undertaken diligent efforts to ensure accuracy, there is no guarantee of the accuracy of no errors, omissions or typographical errors. Any slights of people or organizations are unintentional. The author and publisher shall have no liability or responsibility to any person or entity and hereby disclaim all liability, including without limitation, liability for consequential damages regarding any claim, loss or damage that may be incurred, or alleged to have been incurred, directly or indirectly, arising out of the information provided in this book.

Copyright © 2016 by Luke Gregory

Contents

The Fact and Fiction of Passive Income 8
    So why would I quit my job to work for myself then? 13
    Because you CAN do this. 15
    This is where the unicorns come back into the picture 16
    You have to stay positive because there's a chilling truth about negativity: 18
    Believe in yourself. 19
    My inner warrior has beaten back the fearful side of my nature from atop a glorious unicorn steed, now what? 19
    So what's the rest of this book going to look like? 21

Step 1: Understand Who You Are 25
    How do I know what kind of person I am? 26
    It's time for some science 28
    Here come the unicorns 30
    Yeah right, how does that work? 32
    Internalizing/Externalizing: 33
    Introverted/Extroverted: 35
    Passive/Active: 37
    Participant/Observer: 38
    So what does all of this mean? 39
    I'm still confused ... about everything. 40
    Now that you know yourself better, it's time to take a look at your life 42
    I don't have kids, and I don't need to bond with my family ... 45

Step 2: Find Your Passion 47
   Sabrina loved anthropology when she wasn't fully engaged with it. 52
   Sabrina used what she learned in school to complement her work as a writer. 53
   Sabrina knew she was heading in the wrong direction, but she ignored it for a long time. 54
   Okay, so how exactly do I find my passion 55
   Look at successful people to learn how to be a success 58
   Oh no, the unicorns are back! 59
   And now it's time for the horses 61
   Why shouldn't I set plans by my big dreams? 63
   But that doesn't mean you're not going to fail from time to time. 64
   This seems like so much work! Do I need to find my passion for doing this? 65
   Why is it worth it? 67
   You're not going to feel any better about doing this than you do about your nine-to-five job if it isn't something you care about beyond the earning capacity. 67
   I'll never get out of debt 71
   You have to be unscrupulous to be a millionaire 72
   Earning lots of money takes too much work 73
   Work is something you do just to pay the bills 74
   Getting by is all I can ever hope for 75
   The deck is stacked against those who aren't already wealthy 76
   You can't make money doing something you love 76

Okay, now I know why I should do this. How do I do it? 78

Step 3: From Passion to Product 79

    Different types of income 81

    Passive Income..81

    What does passive income look like? 84

    What are the benefits of passive income? 85

    Why do I need to base a passive-income business in something that I'm passionate about? 86

    Residual Income..90

    Make sure you're using good resources 91

    Active Income 93

    Linear Income 95

    Turning your passion into a viable product 96

    Information-based products 99

    Craft-based products: 103

    Service-based products:..105

    Can't I combine all of these different types of products? 107

    What is your niche? 108

    Effective time leveraging can be about more than higher financial earnings 111

    Referral marketing is an essential aspect of the entire process if you want to be successful 114

    If this is true, why do so many businesses offer bad products? 115

    If you hear hooves, think horses, not unicorns........116

    Referral marketing is about networking more than it's about selling 118

Changing from active to passive income: knowing what role you will play in every step of the process 120

A saturated market is not necessarily a bad thing 124

Deciding when it is time to switch from an active to a passive role 130

Learn how to market your products 134

Becoming wealthy means diversifying 136

Step 4: Creating a Business Plan 138

Executive Summary 141

Products and Services 146

Market Analysis Summary 148

Strategy and Implementation 148

Business Summary 150

Financial Plan 151

Appendix 154

Don't include extraneous information 160

Make sure your reasoning is sound 160

A huge market base is not necessarily a good thing 161

Your financial summary should be realistic 162

Make sure your team accounts for all of your core needs ... 164

Make sure your goals are fully expressed 164

Step 5: Intelligent Expansion 166

My business is doing great, and I'm ready to make massive changes! 168

Determine your growth by the foundation you have already set 169

Proper growth is essential to achieving passive income 171

Expanding your products and services 172
Expansion means that your role within the company has to change..182
Maintaining the founding ideals of the company..................183
Changing infrastructure and resultant needs 183
Disagreements among your core operating staff 184
Customer Service 184
Personnel Changes..185
You're going to need more capital..185

Conclusion 187

The Fact and Fiction of Passive Income

So you've decided to take the plunge and try something new in your professional life. You've been hearing all the hype about internet-based businesses and the ease of generating 'passive' income from home—or a beach on Maui.

There are so many websites, seminars, and e-books available on the topic that the information can be overwhelming. Some say you'll be working 60 hours a week because passive income isn't so passive, others claim that you'll become lazy once your new six-figure income starts rolling in—within the next year to boot!

My favorites are the ones that manage to simultaneously claim you'll be working sixty hours a week while also becoming lazy. And, no matter what, the key to all of these programs seems to be happy thoughts, whether they're mixed with hard work or cocktails on the beach.

I can assure you, the methods in this book are not going to include promises that money will come floating to you from the sky atop a pink unicorn whose magic is powered by your positive thinking. The unicorn will be purple, obviously.

No, unfortunately, the myth about passive income is not true. The Lottery remains the only way to become wealthy by doing nothing. You can take that bet if you want to, but wouldn't you rather bet on yourself instead? Myths are usually based in reality, and the reality is that you can become wealthy by doing something you love. You can't guarantee the lottery, but you can count on yourself.

You can create a passion-based business and bring it to the point where you're earning more money for less direct effort on your part. That is the essence of passive income: structuring your business so that you can leverage your time into higher earnings for fewer hours of direct involvement.

Before you can do this, however, you have to understand the facts about passive income, among other things. You see, there are all sorts of ways you can create a business in which you're doing fulfilling work while building a good income. However, your income won't be passive unless you are taking a passive role in the business. Depending on what you want to do, it may be a while before you can or want to take a passive role. Even then, the passive role isn't as passive as it sounds.

Take a look at the following technical definition to see what I mean:

Passive income is a type of revenue in which the recipient is not materially involved in the business venture which creates the revenue.

The only criteria for passive income is that you cannot be "materially involved" in the business from which you're earning revenue. Being materially involved means that you have either contributed 500 or more hours to the venture within that year or that you are contributing the majority of the work that it takes to sustain the venture.

The term 'passive income' is a technical designation for income specified on your IRS tax forms, and you can only claim it if it meets the above criteria. Every advertisement and flashy marketing scheme on the subject are dead wrong. They'd have you believe that passive income is comprised of the residual earnings from e-books, webinars, websites, and things of that nature. According to these sources, the income is considered passive because you don't have to do very much to earn it once you've created a product and put it up for sale.

To start with, royalty earnings from e-books, patents, and music are not considered passive income by the IRS. You can make a good living from royalty revenues, but it will never be based on passive income. Now, if you were to start an e-book editing business and hire out most of the work, you would be earning passive income. In short, if you make money from a business that is primarily run by your employees, you're earning passive income.

This sounds great, right? That's because it is! The flashy marketing schemes may be wrong on some specifics, but there's a reason they're trying to sell the idea. You can start a business doing something you love, and then grow it until you only have to focus on the aspects of it you enjoy the most. You'll be earning money no matter what, and you can use your extra time to vacation, pursue a hobby, look for investment opportunities, or even start another business!

There's still some myth here, though. While the income is passive, and your role is passive, that doesn't mean you won't be doing any work. That's where the flashy advertising gets it wrong.

You are still responsible for your business. Even though the deckhands are doing most of the work that moves the ship forward, your hand is still on the wheel. The ship might go down if you aren't there to steer, or it might end up at a destination you don't agree with.

It will take time and effort to turn your small business into something that earns passive income. Once you get there, you will still have work to do, and your responsibilities will have changed. It is up to you as to when and how you decide to take a passive role in your company, and we will discuss that in later chapters. For now, just remember that passive income is possible, but it doesn't mean you'll be able to stop working entirely.

So why would I quit my job to work for myself then?

That's an excellent question. Honestly, the only person who can answer that question is the one reading this book right now. Why do you want to quit your job and pursue your own business? Do you want:

- More time with your family?
- The freedom to turn your passion into a career?
- A better sense of financial security?

None of these are good reasons.

If you want more time with your family, that's still going to be an issue when you're juggling clients and trying to stay up on market trends. You can start your endeavor with the best of intentions, only to realize five years later that you forgot to work on your passion while you were taking work to pad your bank account—or even just to pay the bills in the lean months. As for financial security, that's something that is built over time through wise spending and saving practices.

You aren't going to fix these things quickly because all of them take the same exact two things as your business venture to be successful:

- A Plan
- Dedicated and focused effort over a period.

If you want to improve any area of your life, it takes these two things. An organized method of action (a plan), and consistent work towards achieving the result. Anything worth doing usually takes work because we learn through our actions. That's what helps to improve you as a person, which inevitably improves your life, and that's what makes it worth it.

A successful passion-based business isn't impressive because it's based on doing less for more: it's awesome because it's based on you. You run it; you make all the decisions. You get to choose what it looks like and, to a certain extent, how it works. You can structure something that allows you to follow your passions and to learn more about the parts of life that interest you.

Instead of spending eight hours a day plugging away at work that feels meaningless to you, you can work at something that helps you to improve yourself as you improve it. Instead of being stuck in a limited cycle of mind-numbing work, you'll be carried along on a cycle of continuous self-improvement.

If you feel as though you're trapped in a dead-end job, and you are truly ready to make some significant changes in your life, keep reading. If you're under or unemployed, and you have a burning desire to find meaningful work, keep reading. If you're facing an illness that leaves you mostly housebound, but you refuse to let that stop you, keep reading. If you have a family, you not only want to support but to inspire, keep reading. Why?

Because you CAN do this.

Know that. Close your eyes and believe. Literally. Get a visual of your ideal self. Take note of how you're dressed, how you hold yourself, what you're doing, where you're living, what your life is like. Feel deep down inside your gut that you have everything you need to be successful, because you do.

This is where the unicorns come back into the picture

The secret is hardly a secret anymore, and a lot of people are tired of hearing about how positivity can save the world. But what if it could? We're learning so much about the human mind and body these days, and there are a lot of techniques for stress management that tout the benefits of positive thinking.

According to a May 2016 Psychology Today article entitled "Rewrite Your Life," there are significant benefits to changing the way you look at things. Many psychological resources note the importance of your internal dialogue when it comes to framing your life. It's a normal human inclination to make minor shifts in our life story that cause us to interpret failure—or similarly shaming situations—as having helped us to build character and wisdom. If we don't go too far with this, it can allow us to overcome difficult situations with more grace and to continue moving forward even when we fail.

Change your story. Don't look at yourself as a victim, don't blame outside circumstances when problems arise. Tell yourself that setbacks are only challenges, and a challenge is simply life's way of sending you new opportunities to grow. Maybe you'll learn something new from those challenges, and that new information will spin your business off into a new and beautiful direction. Think of these new opportunities like a raise. It's time to move up to the next level. It must be because life is teaching you something new—pay attention to what it is.

Failure is simply the opportunity to begin again, this time, more intelligently.
– Henry Ford

You have to stay positive because there's a chilling truth about negativity:

Being negative will keep you from seeing and grasping new opportunities.

This may all sound corny to you, but you'll never get your business off the ground if you can't stay positive. If you let stress and fear stand in your way, you'll make poor decisions based off of faulty logic. Fear can also cause you to live in a dreamland, envision how beautiful your future will be, but do little to create that vision—this is still falling victim to faulty logic. If you give in to these tendencies, things may work out for a little while. At a certain point, however, all the little mistakes you made could add up to a failed business. You're going to experience stress from time to time, and you'll have to figure out ways to handle it so that it doesn't lead to bad choices for your business. Meditation and taking walks often help, but to let go of stress you have to access your inner warrior.

We all have one, each unique to ourselves. This is just another way of telling you to change your story, or to keep the right mindset, or to fake it until you make it. In essence, they're all saying that you should:

Believe in yourself.

It all starts there. Believe in your ability to do it, and you'll find yourself making a way when no one else can even see where you're going. But you'll know because you're a warrior with a plan—and you're riding a unicorn. Now that's positive thinking.

My inner warrior has beaten back the fearful side of my nature from atop a glorious unicorn steed, now what?

The next step is, to be honest with yourself about what you want. If you had more time, what would you do with it? Do you want to pursue something artistic? Is there a cause you feel passionately about? Have you always dreamed of writing novels, or becoming a freelance journalist? Do you love the world of finance and want to share it with others? Figure out your niche, and then you can start brainstorming about how to earn income with it through a small business.

You have to know who you are and what you want your life to look like before you can truly know what kind of business you want to run. You can most certainly create a passion-based business that you can eventually turn into passive income, but it will be your decision when you decide to take that role. Taking a passive role means that you won't be actively engaged with your business anymore, and we will explore what that might look like a little later in the book.

By now you should have learned several things:

-Passive income is a technical IRS term that does NOT apply to internet-based revenue streams.

-You can earn a real income from a passion-based business, but it WILL take work.

-You should not start a new business to solve problems that don't start at work.

Self-improvement and new business ventures take the same two things:

-A plan

-Dedicated and focused effort over a period

> *Changing how you see yourself and your life will help you move past fear and make better decisions.*

If failure is approached as a lesson, you will be able to use it as a stepping stone instead of feeling as though you've hit a wall.

You are a warrior riding a unicorn, and you CAN do this.

So what's the rest of this book going to look like?

This book will outline five basic steps you need to take to get started. It probably won't be easy, but it will be worth it. The steps are:

- *Understand Who You Are*: If you're going to do this, you need to know if you're ready. Can you make room in your life for something that's going to take long hours, probably in addition to the hours you already work at your day job? Are you the kind of person who can successfully see this through and continue to grow it? If not, can you make life changes to become that kind of person? If you know more about who you are, you will be able to make better choices as you build your business because you will know what you want.

- *Find Your Passion*: We covered this a moment ago when you were asked to think about what you wish to pursue passionately. This section will offer in-depth information about how to know what you want to do. You will have an easier time keeping your business going through the rough times if it is based on something that you are passionate about. While you can skip this step, and the even the first one, you will be missing out on the primary purpose of this book: to create a better you by building a passion-based business and putting you in control of your financial future.

- *From Passion to Product*: This section will teach you how to take the information from steps 1 and 2 and use it to find a niche and create a product. It will offer in-depth information on different types of income earnings and various aspects of effective marketing and business practices.

- *Creating a Business Plan*: This may seem relatively straightforward, but planning is an essential part of the process. This section will not only help you create a viable business plan; it will show you how to tailor that plan as you go along. You'll learn how to set goals and refine goals as you progress efficiently.

- *Intelligent Expansion*: Expansion is another way of saying growth. This chapter will teach you how to successfully grow your business over time while taking into account how it will change the structure of your business, and your role within it.

- *Conclusion*: This is a very short chapter that will wrap up the book and provide a list of the most valuable information to take from the pages within.

Each section will contain subsections that go into more detail about what you need to know and do, at every stage of the process. Throughout the book, I will address the role of passive income and how you can switch from an active to a passive role.

Now that we have a roadmap for where we're going let's get started.

Step 1: Understand Who You Are

Not everyone has what it takes to own their own business. Many people try and fail. Others try and fail repeatedly. The ones who make it are the ones who keep trying. What determines this phenomenon? Why do some of us stare failure in the face and laugh while others shed a tear and walk away?

Psychology, that's why.

Our brains are complex little machines comprised of overarching (conscious) and under-arching (subconscious) networks of thought. These networks work together to incorporate the whole that is you. The first thing you need to do to be successful is determined what kind of person you are. How do you approach challenges? How do you feel when dealing with other people? Are you confident, or do you shy away? These things are determined by the complex interplay of your mind, so you need to know yourself very well if you're going to rely on yourself as the sole means of earning an income.

This is because every step of your business is going to require that you make choices. These choices will determine what your business looks like, what role you play within it, and therefore what role your business will play in your life. This includes the choice to switch from an active to a passive role, and every choice it will take to get there.

While you shouldn't expect to be happy every second that you're working on your business, you don't want to build a business that won't bring you joy. You will better know how to structure you venture throughout every part of the process if you know what you want in life. To know what you want, you have to know what kind of person you are.

How do I know what kind of person I am?

Self-reflection is key here. Pay attention to how you interact with the world around you. Take note of the nature of thoughts that you have when you're talking with other people or going about your day. If your thoughts are overwhelmingly negative, that's going to be a problem. You need to understand your personality. Once you understand yourself better, you can go about making changes wherever you feel they're necessary.

This isn't going to happen overnight. Much like your business, self-improvement takes a plan and consistent effort towards realizing that plan. It sounds like a lot of work, so why do it?

If you aren't seeking to become better as you build your business, then you're not building the skills you need to be successful in the next step. Running a business, especially if you're going to bring it to the point of passive income, requires self-discipline and the willingness to learn new skills as you go.

You have to know who you are to understand how to run your business best and grow with it. If you're exceptionally outgoing, then you would probably make different marketing and networking decisions than someone who is more reserved. Maybe you're shy, but you know you want to run a business that will put you in the limelight.

Overcoming your shyness would then become a personal goal that aligns with your business goals.

It's time for some science

Everyone has a unique personality that is comprised of the interaction between their deep subconscious, limbic system, and conscious mind. The deep subconscious controls autonomic functions such as heart rate and breathing, and it also plays a role in memory formation.

The limbic system acts as a bridge between your conscious mind and deep subconscious, and it is physically situated between the two. It interprets emotional responses based on memory input from the deep subconscious, working together to create your reality and how you respond to it. These impulses will tell you to react with peace or fear based on the memory input your limbic system uses to process and output information.

This part of your brain also determines how you feel about yourself and others because the limbic system is what allows you to distinguish between yourself and other people. This is the nurture part of your makeup, and it's mostly based on the interactions you had with your parents and those individuals who composed your primary relationships when you were younger.

The conscious mind comprises the nature side of your makeup. It is the way in which you will interact with the world based on the neural input provided by your limbic system. The way your conscious mind works is determined by genetics, but it operates in coordination with your limbic system to give you a range of possible composite personalities.

This is how a person changes throughout life. The genetically determined mechanisms in the conscious brain ebb and flow based on how a person is living and thinking, but the basic foundation of the personality is determined by the limbic system. This is because the limbic system tells you how to respond emotionally based on how you have reacted in the past.

So, if you feed your limbic system new input, you can change the way it responds in the future. Your thoughts and actions are a self-feeding loop that will continue to grow upon themselves. If you want to change the nature of your thoughts, input new information into your brain. Think in a different way and, over time, the new method of thinking will become natural.

Here come the unicorns

We've all heard of mantras and affirmations. If you haven't, how did you miss the new-age craze? Tsk tsk, you're going to have to pay better attention to markets if your business is ever going to be a success.

If you haven't heard of mantras and affirmations, essentially these are positive statements you repeat to yourself daily to improve your life. They do work, and if you paid attention to the above psychology lesson, you'd see how.

Your limbic system interprets and outputs information based on memories of how you have responded to similar situations in the past. So, if you feed your limbic system new input, you can change the way it responds in the future. Your thoughts and actions are a self-feeding loop that will continue to grow upon themselves. If you want to change the nature of your thoughts, input new information into your brain. Think in a different way and, over time, the new method of thinking will become natural.

You're telling your brain how you want to think and feel about yourself and others. As speaker and Reverend, Joel Osteen would say, you're reprogramming your thoughts. You're using your conscious mind to direct how your subconscious mind tells you to feel. As your subconscious mind accepts the new information, it will direct your conscious mind differently. This will not happen overnight. With focused and dedicated effort, you'll be able to improve the nature of your thoughts and—consequently—your personality.

Yeah right, how does that work?

Your conscious mind is an interplay of four fundamental and genetically determined factors that work together to create your overall personality. The input from your limbic system is translated through the lens of these four factors.

Think of it this way: your immediate response to a situation, on a wordless level, is your limbic system. This is how you feel. How you act based on how you feel is determined by the four factors that comprise your conscious mind. To understand yourself better, you'll need to understand these four factors. Then you can decide what kind of person you find yourself to be, and whether or not you might have to do some reprogramming to achieve the success you want in life.

Each of these four factors come in groupings of two terms. The two terms represent different aspects of the same genetically determined personality factor. You will never be all or one of the other. Each factor is determined by a mix of the two terms. As such, you might be 30% introverted and

70% extroverted, totaling 100%. These numbers can and do shift throughout your life, which marks transitions and changes in your overall personality.

If you want to be successful in your new venture, you have to know how to structure a business that will work for you. You have to set goals and create a structure based on who you are. Otherwise, you're going to burn out. Understanding how personality works, and how you can tailor your business to your personality and vice-versa, is essential to creating a viable organization. So, let's get into it.

The four factors that determine your overall personality

Internalizing/Externalizing:

This facet of personality has to do with how your conscious mind interprets the feelings your limbic system associated with the idea of the other. The other being people who are not you. Let's say you're an internalizer. When you have a friendly and positive interaction with another person, your mind will interpret the source of those emotions as being from within yourself. An externalizer, on the other hand, will understand these emotions as having arisen from the other person and being projected onto the self. An internalizer derives the feelings of love from others as an internal source; an externalizer seeks these feelings of love and support from an external source (others).

If you're more of an internalizer, you won't need to rely so much on outside support to keep you motivated. This is not to say that you'll never need it, but you can accomplish a lot simply by setting and adhering to your standards. Your assumption of love from others doesn't require other people to maintain itself as much as an externalizer's will. However, you will have to keep yourself motivated. Speak lovingly to yourself, don't pressure yourself to succeed outside of achievable standards. Don't set yourself up for failure. Create a strong internal support system that will help to carry you through rough times by incorporating and achieving personal goals.

If you're an externalizer, you should build an external support system. Join a professional association for small businesses and go to meetings. Set goals that involve getting valid client and user feedback, but remember to learn what you can from the negative reviews and let them go. Create an inner circle of people who support you and your dreams, and keep negative people out of this circle. There is always room for honest critical feedback; there is no room for naysayers.

Introverted/Extroverted:

An introverted person is not necessarily shy, nor is an extrovert always bold and assertive. Essentially, an introvert creates their vision of the world from a self-oriented position. An extrovert derives their vision of the world from others. Essentially, an introvert is focused inwardly, and an extrovert is focused outwardly.

If you're more introverted, the measure of success from your business should reflect that. Allow for your work to help you meet personal as well as professional goals, and you'll find yourself singing every time you meet one of them. Maybe your business isn't about changing the world so much as it's about changing you, and there's absolutely nothing wrong with that.

An extroverted person, on the other hand, will likely want to set goals that are not as inclined towards personal self-development. The growth of the business and client relationships would probably be a better focus for someone who is more extroverted.

This is not to say that more extroverted people won't undergo personal changes and growth, just that it will occur under different circumstances for them. The same goes for introversion. Your business will still grow if your focus is turned more towards personal development. Keep in mind that this isn't just about growing a business, it's about building your business. Know where you're starting from and you'll have a better idea of where you want to go.

Passive/Active:

Passive and active have to do with our sense of protection. Are we the protector (active), or are we the one who needs protecting (passive)?

An active person is more likely to go out and do something to effect change, while a passive person is more liable to contemplate the world around them and see where change could be enacted. If you're passive, you're going to have to modify the balance of your personality. It's excellent to see where new opportunities occur, or where changes could and should be made. However, it means little if you can't take the initiative to make the changes.

You can accomplish this by taking action on your thoughts. Start small, maybe don't even start with your business. Take steps in your day-to-day life to become more active. When you're feeling more confident in your ability to take action, then you can turn your thoughts and your deeds back to your business. Or, maybe starting your business is what will help you to become more active. Figure out what will work for you, and do it!

If you have an actively inclined personality, you'll need to take steps to make sure you're not forcing yourself on others. Slow down; not everything has to happen right away. Change takes time, remember?

Participant/Observer:

This facet of your personality determines how you relate to your reality. A participant is more likely to become emotionally involved with other people, creating and maintaining dynamic relationships that allow the participant to actively engage in the world through feelings and emotions.

An observer is more likely to take in the world from a distance. These people will stand back and watch others, engaging with the world through the lens of their feelings and emotions. A participant is more likely to act out their emotions, while an observer is more likely to reflect on them.

Both of these are essential qualities for business. If you find yourself to be more of an observer, then you might want to take to meditating as a way of clearing your thoughts and organizing your ideas. If you're more of a participant, you'll want to create a business that keeps you engaged with others.

So what does all of this mean?

If you're going to do this right, you have to know where you're starting from. Let's say you're a passive, introspective, extroverted, observer. You like to think about things more than other people, you're less likely to take risks, more likely to spot market trends, and would probably enjoy working with others to a limited extent.

You have strength in spotting market trends, but you are weak in that you may not take enough risks. However, you probably work better leading a team than on your own because you're also extroverted and will feed off of the group input. You can work with your strengths while you find ways to increase your ability to take measured risks in your business. You might even consider hiring someone to a consulting position who will help you identify and take appropriate risks.

Now you can see why it's important to know who you are. If you start a business without understanding what works for you, you're building failure into your future. You have to know what you're capable of doing, what will make your business largely enjoyable for you, and how you need to grow personally to continue to grow professionally.

I'm still confused ... about everything.

Okay, so let's take it back to your warrior self. You're still sitting on top of that beautiful unicorn. In this scenario, your warrior is the conscious mind, and your unicorn is the limbic system.

It might seem like the unicorn should direct where you'll be going and how fast you're going to get there. While you're certainly limited by the capabilities of your unicorn, ultimately the warrior holds the reigns. The qualities possessed by you will determine what actions you take when, say, your unicorn gets spooked by a snake and takes off running. Will you react quickly, or will panic set in and send you and your unicorn careening off the edge of a cliff?

No, because you are in control.

Grab the reigns, and tell your unicorn where you want to go. You are the warrior, and you are in control. Remember to take care of your unicorn, too. Don't push him too hard. Treat him lovingly, and feed him—otherwise, someone's getting a visit from PETA.

Treat yourself with love and respect, and you'll feel loved and respected. That's your fuel: that's the essence of positive thinking. If you want to manifest your dreams, you have to fine-tune your mind because your mind is what shapes your reality. If you want to keep it running smoothly, then you have to understand and work with its parts.

Now that you know yourself better, it's time to take a look at your life

So you've sat around with some candles and chanted and hummed until the glories of your inner self-rose to the surface and said 'hello!'. Or maybe you just did some thinking. Either way, you're probably wondering what comes next.

Now that you know what to expect from yourself, you have to look at what to expect from your environment. Are you in a position where you can quit work today? If you did that, would you be motivated enough to start your business? Do you have a family to support, and does that family support you?

These are only a few questions you could ask yourself. Do an honest and thorough assessment of your life. What does it look like now, what do you want it to look like, and how could you bridge the gap from here to there?

If you're doing this right, you'll be using what you learned about yourself in the previous section to process and sort the information in this one. Are you unhappy right now? Try to pinpoint why. Sometimes what seems like the problem is only a symptom of something deeper.

For instance, maybe you want more time with your family. You work too much these days, and you never seem to find enough hours for true bonding experiences with your loved ones. You might be right. Work may be the problem. Or not.

Some people don't work at all, and they still never spend time with their families. Others spend time with their family, but they don't spend that time doing things that would build strong bonds between them.

When it comes to time with the household, it is quality and not quantity that matters. Relationships, no matter what form they take, require work. You have to consistently try to develop and maintain bonds with your loved ones by meeting them on common ground. Show an interest in who they are and what they like to do, and they will likely show you the same in return.

So, if you're starting your own business to have more time with your family, then consider including your family in the process. Figure out what your kids like to do, and find ways they can help. Talk with your spouse and see if there's any aspect of your work to which they might like to contribute. It's all about finding creative solutions to incorporate the various aspects of your life and desires into the business you're building.

That's why it's important to know what your life looks like now, and what you want it to look like in the future. Maybe you're starting an online Etsy store that sells decorative pillows. Your daughter loves flowers, and she loves to draw. Perhaps you could make an entire line of floral design pillows, all of which follow patterns you asked your daughter to create for the line. Maybe you discover that your other daughter has a hidden love for programming and computers. Could she design an app that allows your customers to design their pillows for custom orders? Once they've done so, will you need your other daughter to translate those designs into a viable pattern you can work with? Now you've encouraged both your daughter's passions, enhanced your business, and also given your children invaluable experience in the world of small business—plus, you got them to work together on something for once! This is what real bonding looks like the mutual acceptance and nurturance of growth within each other.

I don't have kids, and I don't need to bond with my family

The above is merely an example of how you go from a general goal to the specifics of how you are going to achieve it. Spend some time reflecting on your current life and see where you do want to make room for the things you care about. You'll need to keep all of this in mind when you get to the planning phase of your business so that you can produce a workable blueprint for the year (or years) ahead.

There's another crucial element to this as well. No one lives in a bubble. Your actions and decisions do have an effect on the other people in your life. While you should never cater to someone else's expectations or harsh criticisms, it is polite to take them into account when making decisions. This will ensure that your environment is supportive. No matter how you derive your sense of self-worth (from within or without), you will be affected by the attitudes of the people around you. If you show them that they're a part of this process as well, the road ahead should travel much more smoothly because everyone's needs are being met.

We've learned a lot in this chapter. We've covered the core components that work together to comprise personality, and we've taken a look at how you can collaborate with those various elements to create a business that works for you. We've also discussed how you can work to creatively incorporate different aspects of your life into your business. This kind of endeavor isn't something people do because they want to get rich quickly. It's a method of self-improvement that will allow you to become your ideal self while creating your perfect life.

In essence, the riches you gain will be counted in more than money. This is an important thing to keep in mind. You should count your growth in dollars and sense. Everything you learn has value. Every step you take will improve who you are. Every personal and professional relationship you nurture will contribute to your quality of life. If you can learn to count your success by these standards, you'll go a long way towards improving your mindset and creating your ideal life.

Step 2: Find Your Passion

So you've spent some time getting to know yourself better, you've thought about how you want to incorporate your life into your business and your business into your life, but you're still left wondering just what it is you're going to do.

Maybe you had a plan. You went to college, you worked hard, you graduated and went on to get your masters and Ph.D. Now you're cruising through your field, wondering if you worked so hard just to live your life on autopilot. Where did you go wrong? Isn't that what you were supposed to do? Why don't you feel more fulfilled, you followed the path laid out for you by society? You loved your field of study in school, most of the time, but now that you're doing it something feels off.

We all go through periods of time in our lives when we *feel like we're not on the right path.*

Here's the thing about that: there's no such thing as not being on your path.

Think about it. Your path is your linear progression through life. The road to success is loopy, often folding back in on itself, but your overall path through life occurs as one day gives way to the next. You don't stop aging when you stop loving what you do—if you did, the world would be full of youthful misery. You can't fall off your path in life, but sometimes you do come to an intersection. You can keep moving forward, or you can veer off to the left or the right.

These are the times when we become confused and feel as though we're lost. You're not lost; you only need to decide which way to go. Can you work through your angst to find happiness in your career once again? Maybe you should go straight, but tailor what you're carrying on your journey, so you don't feel so over-burdened. Maybe you can make changes within your career to find the happiness you seek. If this is you, congratulations: you probably don't need to finish reading this book!

If this isn't you, and I have a feeling that it's not, then you have some thinking to do. You see, before you make a choice as to which way to turn you need to pause and evaluate where you've been.

What led you to this intersection? What did you like about your journey so far, and what would you like to avoid repeating? Think of this intersection as an opportunity that life has sent you. If you're unhappy with your story, this is the time to change it—no matter which direction you choose.

You can't make an informed decision about what path will bring you more happiness if you don't know what brings you joy. Think about your career: why did you choose it? Are these reasons still valid for you? If so, why are you unhappy? Can you find a way to translate what you love about your career into your own business?

To illustrate what this might look like in real life, take the following vignette into account:

Sabrina studied anthropology in school. She always wanted to be a writer, but circumstances and fear led her to study something else. She fell in love with anthropology which, as it turns out, entails lots of writing! Then it came time to do her first field research. She had invested three years of study in this program, and she was so excited to be out in the real world using all she had learned.

Sabrina soon ran into trouble while doing her field research. She learned that being the researcher is not the same as reading the research. She didn't feel right about it, and she didn't like how she was engaging with people and the world. The whole thing left her feeling incomplete and lost. But she had invested so many years into this, so it must just be nerves. How could she let her teachers, her family, and her friends down by failing? Against her better judgment, Sabrina finished her research and returned to school. She didn't do well.

No matter what, she couldn't shake the feeling that something was wrong. She came to detest her field of study, and eventually she dropped out without earning her degree.

Years would pass before she realized that it wasn't that something was wrong with anthropology or anthropologists, it was simply that this was not how she enjoyed engaging with the world.

Sabrina went on to become the writer she had always wanted to be. She used all of the skills and knowledge she gained through her studies to become a better writer. Her unique background often led to a form of expression that many found to be new and refreshing.

There are a few key things that you need to pull out from this example:

- Sabrina loved anthropology when she wasn't fully engaged with it.
- Sabrina used what she learned in school to complement her work as a writer.
- Sabrina knew she was heading in the wrong direction, but she ignored it for a long time.

Sabrina loved anthropology when she wasn't fully engaged with it.

There is a difference between passion and interest. When you're interested in something, you'll probably read a lot about it and want to talk about it. When you're passionate about something, you'll want to live and breathe it. You'll approach it with a level of emotion that doesn't seem to apply in other areas of your life.

If someone were to insult the father of modern anthropology in front of Sabrina, she would probably shrug it off. If someone were to insult her favorite author, well, they're fighting words! You will be able to recognize your passion the same way that you understand your personality: by paying attention to how you engage with the world and respond to different situations. If you're paying enough attention to yourself, you'll begin to recognize where you're passionate and where you simply have a passing interest.

Sabrina used what she learned in school to complement her work as a writer.

Your interests may not be what you focus on, but they can complement your passion. Think of it this way, a science fiction writer either has two passions—totally possible—or a passion for one thing and an interest in another. In the combination of these things, something new is born. Much like your personality, it is the way you combine your interests and passions that will allow you to create something as unique as you are.

There's an easy real-life example to use here. Scientist Neil Degrasse Tyson has a passion not only for science but also for sharing science in a way that makes it a more mainstream part of society. Tyson worked for years as a scientist before he branched out into creating a public image that allowed him to share his passion with the world in a new way. Now he writes books, hosts a popular talk show about science, and engages in some other projects that promote interest in and engagement with various fields of science.

Sabrina knew she was heading in the wrong direction, but she ignored it for a long time.

Sabrina ignored her gut instincts, and she suffered for it. That last year before she dropped out was rough. She questioned herself and her value regularly; she tried to work only to feel sick over every word she wrote. Even writing had become something dreaded because she was using her passion to express something she didn't believe in.

If you feel something such as this—drained, depressed, alone, empty—you need to seriously re-evaluate your life. Somewhere along the road, you may have taken a wrong turn; or you continued forward when you should have turned. It's not about taking the road less traveled because the road is yours. No one has ever walked down it before.

Sabrina worried so much about letting others down that she never considered how she might be letting herself down. No, it's not okay to skip out on your obligations. It is normal to reconsider your life goals and change them if you feel it's in your best interest. What other people think doesn't matter. Don't choose a path because you want to be a maverick, or because you think it will please the people around you. You can't make the people around you happy; only they can do that. And only you can do what it takes to make yourself happy.

If you're lost on a lonely road, you should know that you aren't alone. A lot of people have been where you are, all throughout history and into the present. What you do now will come to define you in the years to come. Now is the time to pull on every experience that's ever taught you something about life, and use it to find your way. Find your passion, and you'll know in which direction you should move.

Okay, so how exactly do I find my passion

A good place to start is by enjoying the works that were born of other people's passions. Seek out music, movies, books, projects, blogs, historical accounts, or anything that exemplifies real passion. You will be able to recognize a passionate work by how it makes you feel, and you can find passionate people because they are often known as masters of their field or craft.

The reason is simple. When someone expresses themselves in a genuinely passionate way, it results in something that can reach others on a deep and meaningful level. This is where passion comes from, and it always recognizes its own. If you want to awaken your passion, then you can start by feeding it with other people's.

This goes for who you hang out with too. Surround yourself with passionate people. Create an environment that is full of emotional expression (no, don't turn your relationship into a soap opera—there's a difference between drama and passion). Before long, you'll notice that your creative side is waking up, your passions are coming to the surface. That's because you're actively feeding that part of yourself. That's the funny thing about passion; if you feed it, it will grow.

Over time you might notice a pattern. Sure things may begin to repeat themselves within your growing library of passionate creation. Follow that thread; it will likely lead you to what you're trying to learn about yourself.

Once you've followed that thread and discovered some things you feel excited about, spend time doing them. As we learned with Sabrina, sometimes you have to be actively engaged in an activity before you know exactly how you feel about it. Devote some time to it as a hobby before you begin thinking about how to make it a career. If you lose interest after a while, you may need to keep exploring other options.

Maybe you don't need to find your passion; maybe you already know what it is. Maybe you've been working at it for a long time now, but things are beginning to feel lackluster. What about that? Does passion wax and wane like that?

Yes, it does. Passion is like a marriage: sometimes you are totally in love, at times you hate each other. Most of the time, you're somewhere between the two. If you're going to work in your passion, sometimes you will resent it or become bored with it. This isn't a sign that you have lost your passion, but it may be a sign that it's time for you to expand it.

Let's look at the example of Neil Degrasse Tyson again. He worked in his passion for a good portion of his life, and at a certain point he used everything his passion had taught him to take it to the next level. Maybe you're at the intersection, but you don't need to go left or right. Perhaps you simply need to walk forward in a new way.

We will discuss this in more detail in the final chapter of this book which deals specifically with expanding your business. For now, just keep in mind that you may not have to completely change your life to figure out how to earn income from your passion.

Look at successful people to learn how to be a success

Just as you can use other people's passions to help awaken your own, you can also become more successful by paying attention to successful people.

If your measure of success is a certain dollar amount, then pay attention to the habits and business practices of wealthy people.

If you want to become the next big e-book author, look into currently successful authors.

It doesn't matter what you want to accomplish regarding success; you'll have an easier time achieving it if you have an example to help you set standards for yourself. Take into account what you want your life to be like. If you want to earn a lot of money, but you don't want to work long hours, then don't look into workaholic billionaires. Find people who have both the lifestyle and level of success you desire, then go about figuring out how they got there and how you can do the same.

Oh no, the unicorns are back!

You probably thought you were safe. "She's talking about science more and more, that should keep the unicorns at bay!" you said to yourself. Silly reader, unicorns love science.

Earlier you were asked to visualize what you want your life to be like. While it seems like mystical hokum, it can be a healthy psychological trick that helps keep you motivated.

It can also help you figure out what your passion is.

So I want you to do this again. This time, however, visualize multiple scenarios. Make a list of everything you think you ought to pursue. Work through this list, one visualization at a time. See yourself doing the task day after day. Think through the details each life would be like, and who you would be. Pay attention to how each one makes you feel. Do you get excited? Do you find yourself smiling, or is your stomach doing the twist?

Use this to guide you through the decision-making process. This is where your self-knowledge will come in handy again. If you want to trust how you feel, you have to know yourself well enough to understand what your emotional responses mean for you. Are you a nervous kind of person? Then your stomach twisting in queasy knots might be a signal that you've hit on your passion. Only you can discern what your feelings are trying to tell you. While you should seek advice from others, this is one of those situations where your gut instincts should weigh more heavily than anything another person has to say.

And now it's time for the horses

Unicorns are magical and mythical beings; horses exist outside of our imaginations. In this situation, horses represent logic. Visualization can go too far. There's a big difference between visualizing an ideal future and daydreaming. Daydreaming is important, but it can also be detrimental.

Envisioning the possible long-term rewards of your work can help to orient your mindset towards delayed gratification. Everything is instant these days, and our brains have become used to a quick-response rewards system. It's not like playing a video game; you're not going to level up at predictable intervals—and sometimes you'll do the expected work but get unexpected results. You can help yourself stay on track by periodically reminding yourself of what you're gaining. This is a healthy way to use visualization.

When you're doing this, don't stop at the material rewards because this will keep you stuck in a very limited way of thinking. There are other tangible rewards to running your own passion-based business, such as: gaining professional standing; increasing skills that you enjoy doing; expanding your knowledge by taking courses or seeking professional certifications; mastering a craft; becoming increasingly self-disciplined.

The point is to make sure that you're not only visualizing what that life would look like on the outside. Make sure you are also looking at who you're becoming based on your current choices. When you're considering possible futures, take note of how you feel about the different skills you'll have earned to get to that point. This can help you to differentiate better between choices when trying to find your passion, and it can contribute to keeping you motivated if you've already started. Repetitive tasks become easier when you can identify them with their long-term rewards.

Healthy visualization should allow you take a flight of fancy within the boundaries of the work you're willing to do to accomplish your goals. It's okay to dream of the boundless possibilities; it's not okay to set plans by them. If you're setting plans, do so off of visualizations based in the reality of the work you can feasibly do.

Why shouldn't I set plans by my big dreams?

The reason for this is simple. Within the study of logic, there's something called Positive Outcome Bias. This occurs when people think they are more likely to succeed because they have imagined the best possible outcome to a situation. This causes them to identify so heavily with this possibility that they discount or ignore other, more likely, outcomes.

Don't do this.

Visualize what you want, but understand that the steps you take to get there may bring you to a different destination—and even the steps themselves may change. Don't think that, just because your passionate about what you're doing, you don't need to base your efforts on a sound basis of reason and planning. There may be a lot you have to do between the beginning of your efforts and that final result. Every step of the way will help you to grow into who you need to be to reach this final stage. And, as they say, every ending is simply a new beginning in disguise. Once you reach your ideal place, you might just find yourself at another intersection on your path.

If you're going to build residual income from a passion-based endeavor, it is going to take hard work and dedication. You're going to have to turn off the television some nights, you'll have to get up early, you may have to give up some hobbies or even get less sleep. As was explained in the introduction to this book: this is real work. What differentiates it from other tasks is that you will likely find a higher level of fulfillment from it, and it puts you in control of your income and your life.

But that doesn't mean you're not going to fail from time to time.

While there will be more detail about this in the next chapter, which will teach you about writing business plans, you may have to engage in effective methods of earning income before you can build up the aspects that will bring in money while you're not actively working. Everything worth doing takes time, and there is always a chance you will fail.

Failure is nothing more than an opportunity to learn from your mistakes and try again. With every failure, you will learn something new. Don't think that, just because you've grown and you're pursuing your passions; you can't fail. Learn to handle failure gracefully, instead, and you'll find that it cannot keep you down.

Dream big, visualize realistically, plan for multiple outcomes, and learn to fail gracefully. If you can do these things, all you need is a little hard work to be successful. It may take time, but you'll get there—and you'll have fun every step of the way.

This seems like so much work! Do I need to find my passion for doing this?

No, you don't. You could skip this step entirely, but let me ask you something. Why are you doing this?

In the introduction we discussed why endeavoring to earn residual income from an internet-based business isn't something you should do because you're trying to solve problems that don't source from work.

If you want to have more money to save for retirement, that's great, but you can earn that in many different ways. It also won't matter how much you bring in if you aren't effectively managing your money.

More time with your family isn't going to happen unless you make it happen, no matter what you're doing.

If you want to do work you're passionate about, that's not going to fall from the sky. You have some work to do to get there, but it is worth it—and you CAN do it.

Why is it worth it?

Why are you here, reading this right now? Chances are, something in your life doesn't feel right if you're seeking out options for a change. Here's the bottom line:

You're not going to feel any better about doing this than you do about your nine-to-five job if it isn't something you care about beyond the earning capacity.

Let that sink in. If you're employed full-time right now, you already have enough money coming in to pay the bills and possibly even save a little each month. You may even have job security, as rare as that is these days. Money is great, and who doesn't want to be a millionaire? What's the point of having total financial freedom if you still feel bound to the work it takes to create it?

There are a lot of programs and websites that talk about passive income earnings. Why do you think these websites and programs are using an incorrect term to sell a service for something that doesn't technically exist? They're preying on you. They're taking your dream of financial freedom and turning it into a quick dollar for themselves. That's why some of these sites claim that you'll be able to take it easy on the beach for a good part of every year, they're selling you a dream.

You can make good money doing this, but it will take the time to get there. What's going to keep you motivated in the meantime? Passion.

That's why it's important to figure out what it is you want from life, what you feel you have to offer the world. It becomes too easy to sell false hope when dollar signs are all you're looking at. Don't be like that, and don't judge the people who do take that route.

Instead, only decide to be different. Lead by example. Maybe you truly are passionate about working for yourself, and you want to help others accomplish the same. Be one of the few people who sell an honest program that will help people to gain financial freedom and independence from their business. There are plenty of programs that truly do offer real guidance and support, and you could certainly number among them by bringing your unique personality and experience to the table. For this to be a reality, however, the welfare of your client has to be the bottom line. You have to honestly care that they make it. Otherwise, you risk selling a dream.

Why do people take advantage of others to advance their future? Because they have accepted false beliefs concerning money. A lot of people give into fear-based thinking when it comes to how much they can earn.

Thoughts such as:

- I'll never get out of debt
- You have to be unscrupulous to be a millionaire
- Earning lots of money takes too much work
- Work is something you do just to pay the bills
- Getting by is all I can ever hope for
- The deck is stacked against those who aren't already wealthy
- You can't make money doing something you love

These thoughts might do something worse than keep you from getting started: they might encourage you to make choices that are ethically questionable. If you are only looking at the wealth you can earn, then you're not looking out for yourself. You're not assigning enough value to yourself as a human being because you're not considering your happiness. If you don't care about your happiness, you won't care about other people's either.

While it's true that you can't make another person happy, that doesn't mean you should act in ways that would take advantage of others. You are not responsible for other people's happiness, but you are responsible for your own. Are you going to be happy if you give in to this fear of lack and let it twist you into an unscrupulous millionaire?

You may have answered yes to that. If you did, you're not honest with yourself. Let's go one-by-one through these fearful thoughts and briefly explore what causes them, and why they're wrong. By the end, hopefully, you'll have learned why money shouldn't be the bottom line in any business.

I'll never get out of debt

If you don't address how you got into debt, then you won't. Did you spend frivolously? Did you have to use credit cards to get by? Who taught you that life has to be a hard-scrabble, dollar-by-dollar existence?

It doesn't. While earning residual income does take work, over time you'll build something that keeps money coming in whether or not you're working. Stop focusing on the debt; that fear will stop you. Focus on the opportunities in front of you instead. As we discussed in the introduction, change your story.

Don't see the debt as a burden, see it as a challenge to change your life. Maybe you could use your experiences climbing out of debt to create a program that helps others to do the same. How great would it feel to overcome this struggle, then to reach out your hand to help other struggling people?

That's the real secret: it's not about visualizing your ideal future full of fancy doodads and financial freedom. It's about visualizing how you can live a life that helps yourself while helping others. That's what will bring you real happiness and fulfillment. You can't follow your passion without helping others. Just by lending the example that it can be done, you will be helping others.

You have to be unscrupulous to be a millionaire

Let's be honest; history supports this idea. And that shows in our world today. There are so many problems. But this doesn't have to be true. You can become a solution instead of a problem. Finding your passion will help you to figure out what you care about. If you care about it, you'll approach it differently. If money is not your bottom line, you don't have to be unscrupulous to be successful. You don't have to accept that you will only earn so much because you don't want to take advantage of others. You can earn good money and be honest, but you have to believe that to make it possible.

Earning lots of money takes too much work

You are hard-wired to work. That's why it's so ridiculous that people try to sell a fake service based on the idea that you'll get to a point where you won't have to work anymore. This may sound impressive, but it's not.

You see, you come from a long line of people who had to work hard. If they hadn't, humanity would not have survived as a species. That was the reality for the generations that came before us, and that reality is a little different today. While you can create a business where you don't have to work every day, or you can take an extended vacation every year, you probably don't want to create a life that is all pleasure. Your brain just isn't wired that way.

This is because the pleasure center in your brain will atrophy with overuse. It's kind of like an addiction: the more relaxation you have, the more you need to feel relaxed. We are wired to balance between work and play. Your brain has a built-in rewards system that relies on an exchange of work and plays to maintain optimal functioning. This is why early retirement leads to a shorter lifespan. People need to feel useful to be fulfilled. Don't aim to work again, aim to do work that you love.

Reprogram your thinking to see work for what it is: a privilege. Good, honest work that you enjoy doing is a privilege—not a burden.

Work is something you do just to pay the bills

If survival is all you're thinking about, survival is all you will accomplish. Paying the bills is great, but we are lucky enough to live in a society where we can do more.

You have a real opportunity here to change yourself for the better. By doing so, you will modify the world for the better. Even if you don't seek to directly solve world problems with your work, you will create a happier you.

The thing about happiness is that it's catching. Happy people make better choices.

Work is not just about paying the bills, and it has never been. Our ancestors worked to create a better future for the next generations to come. Don't just pay the bills, build something that will create a better world—that's what work is really about.

So, when you're looking for untapped markets, remember that they're untapped because there's a need there. Why does that need exist, and how can you work to address it? It's not just about making money; it's about providing a valuable service that will improve the world.

Getting by is all I can ever hope for

No, it's not. You are strong, and you are powerful, and you are not the only person who has ever felt like you aren't.

Have the courage to believe something different. Have the courage to forge ahead and make your dreams come true.

By doing so, you will prove to others that it can be done. This alone is a valuable service.

The deck is stacked against those who aren't already wealthy

This is an excuse. It will keep you from even trying to make a better life for yourself. The deck is not stacked against you, but you may have a lot to learn before you can become wealthy. You'll have to learn how to use your money to make more money, how to spend responsibly, how to use credit responsibly, and how to file your taxes correctly, among other things.

Maybe it's not that the game is rigged, maybe you just don't know all of the rules yet. That's okay because you can learn them as you go.

You can't make money doing something you love

Yes, you can. It may seem riskier than the alternative, and you may have to think outside of the box, but it can be done.

Honestly, the only reason it seems risky is that it's unusual. People may think of this as being selfish, but it's more selfish to work solely to earn money. You may be providing a valuable service to your employer, but what if your employer isn't providing a valuable service to the world? The only person you're helping in that scenario is yourself (and your unscrupulous boss).

Our ancestors had to do the work at hand to create the world we live in today. It's our responsibility to build on their hard work by doing some of our own. To accomplish this, we have to think in new ways.

The next step is for people to find work that aligns with causes and actions they feel passionately about. This will change the face of the world. This will create a better world for our descendants. How?

Don't you remember, other people's passions feed your own? It means something to do meaningful work. The more love we put into what we do, the more we will create for ourselves and others.

When you think about it that way, it not only seems possible; it seems necessary. That's right; you have a responsibility to do work that you love! How wonderful is that?

So let's go back to that list of negative, fear-based thoughts and turn them around into what they are:

- Debt is an opportunity to overcome an obstacle and become better.
- I can be a benevolent millionaire.
- Hard work not only earns lots of money, but it is also healthy for my brain.
- I can work to provide a valuable service and pay the bills.
- I can do more than get by; I can create a life of true abundance.
- If I learn the rules of the game, I can easily create and maintain wealth.
- I have a responsibility to make money by doing something that I love.

That sounds better, now doesn't it?

Okay, now I know why I should do this. How do I do it?

We've covered why you should find your passion, and you've learned what to do to change your thinking and prepare yourself to be successful. Now we're getting into the real stuff: the stuff that will help you turn your passion into a business.

The rest of this book will involve the technical information you need to get started and keep going.

Step 3: From Passion to Product

By now you should know a little bit about how you might like to run your business based on your personality, and you should know what you want to pursue regarding your passions and interests. Now let's combine this information and ground it within the real-world possibilities open to you for income earning.

This step will not tell you what to do. It will teach you what you need to know to decide how to begin, to make changes as you go, and to think in a way that will ensure long-term success for you and your business.

From here on out we will deal more with horses than unicorns because steps three thru five will teach you the specific technical information you need to know about business, and how to apply that information to your vision. By the end of this chapter, you will know what you want your actual business to look like. In this step, we will be learning about:

The different types of income and what they mean according to the IRS:

- Passive Income
- Residual Income
- Active Income
- Linear Income

How to combine various types of revenue earnings to create a successful business

- Basic steps to turn a passion into a business
- Determining what type of products you are going to sell
- Figuring out how to make marketing work for you
- Time leveraging and referral marketing
- Knowing the roles you will fulfill in every step of creating your business
- Knowing how and when to switch from active to passive income

So let's get started!

Different types of income

There is so much conflicting and confusing information on the web regarding different types of income. Some people lump residual and passive income together, and others count royalty earnings as a form of passive income—which they are not. Let's go through each type of income, defining each one and exploring the potential it has regarding business opportunities.

Passive Income

*Income that is accrued from a business in which the operator is not materially involved—meaning the operator **works less than 500 hours a year** in that particular business or income collected from a rental property in which the operator does not have direct involvement in the day-to-day management of the property.*

According to the IRS.gov website:

"Passive income can only be generated by a passive activity. **Just because the taxpayer did not work for the income does not mean it is passive**. There are only two sources of passive income:

- A rental activity; or
- A business in which the taxpayer did not materially participate."

The myth: If you don't have to work for the income after the initial effort, it's passive income.

The reality: Passive income is an IRS tax designation that determines how and what you can file as a profit or loss.

Time investment is only one factor in determining whether or not your income is passive.

Let's look at this regarding the real-world applications:

This is **NOT** passive income:

- You have a rental property. You perform the maintenance, collect the rents, and handle the leases.
- You own a business and are directly involved in the creation and marketing of products, management of employees, and the general day-to-day requirements of running the business.
- You are an artist living primarily off of copyright-based royalties (music, e-books, books).
- You are an inventor living primarily off of patent royalties.
- You are an investor living off of dividends and interest earnings from your investments.

According to a lot of information found on the web, anyone of the above scenarios could be considered passive income. However, if you go by the actual IRS designation, none of them are.

This **IS** passive income:

- You own a rental property that is almost entirely managed by employees or a management company.
- You own business, but the majority of the day-to-day work is handled by employees. Your material

involvement comprises less than 500 hours a year of direct work.

So basically, if you publish a bunch of e-books and live off of the royalties, you are not earning passive income. If you start an e-book publishing company, hiring out all of the work, you are earning passive income. This means you would have someone in charge of hiring your editors and writers, someone in charge of marketing, another person in charge of handling comments and Amazon reviews, and someone to oversee all of these people.

As you can see, passive income is not something you can create overnight. Also, you will not be actively involved in the daily reality of creating and selling your product. If you are working in a passion-based business, this could be a good or bad thing. You could see this as something that keeps you from direct involvement in working with your passion, or as something that allows you more time to explore it.

What does passive income look like?

Let's say you love to make jewelry. You start an Etsy store, and it takes off. Soon the demand for your designs is more than you can keep up with. You hire someone to manage your inventory, another person to manage your customer service, people to manufacture your product, and someone to come up with new designs.

You are no longer actively engaged in the process of making anything. However, you have freed up your time so that you can expand and more fully explore your passion. Maybe there's something else you want to explore, consider starting a second business in that area. Maybe you've always wanted to study under a famous designer; now you have the time and money to explore this option. Maybe you still want to design jewelry. You can still do this because it's your business!

You now have the time to focus only on the design. You can spend your days dreaming up beautiful new pieces of jewelry, but leave the actual work of creating and selling them to your employees.

What are the benefits of passive income?

Passive income may take a while to create, but it is the kind of revenue that offers a high level of freedom in your life. You will be earning money no matter what you're doing. You can take a six-month vacation if you want to, and you will still be making money. That is how people become wealthy; they create forms of passive income that allow them the time and freedom to create more forms of passive income. This is how you put your money to work for you, but that does not mean that you will not have to work.

Why do I need to base a passive-income business in something that I'm passionate about?

Honestly, you don't have to. However, the way many people are currently using passive income is becoming increasingly detrimental to our society as a whole. It's creating a marketplace that is flooded with shoddy products, false and manipulative advertising, and a lot of unhappy customers. Let's look at the world of e-books to illuminate this point a little better.

Recently, Amazon.com had to settle a lawsuit in which customers were reimbursed for purchasing poorly-written e-books. Most people reading this have probably bought an e-book from Amazon and wondered just exactly why the author felt they had anything to say on the subject. How does this happen?

Sometimes it's an individual who thought they understood the subject and didn't, but there's something else going on here as well: e-book content mills.

A company will hire ghostwriters, give them a topic, and tell them to deliver an entire e-book within a set amount of time. There is no guarantee that the writer has a knowledge of or passion for the topic, and the company who hired them is only looking for a product to sell.

This is okay if the company is looking to sell a quality product, but some companies are only looking for a quick return of a product geared towards an available market. If they are not doing their due diligence in checking for quality or accuracy, then they are not returning a solid product. That is how you end up with a poorly-written mess.

This is only bad business, and it's also why the internet is full of misinformation. You see, this doesn't just apply to e-books. A lot of times, the websites you read were written by freelancers and ghostwriters. There is a built-in problem here: paying rates for this kind of work are very low. As such, the writer has to deliver a lot of work to sustain them, and this undermines the quality and accuracy of the final product. Either that, or the writer didn't even speak English, to begin with, and what you're reading has been written, edited, and rewritten by multiple people who had no contact with each other during the process.

This is a good thing for you, and here's why: there is an automatic niche in every market for any business—and that niche is quality.

Customer service is coming back, and that is why a passion-based business is a smart idea. People will recognize your passion because your passion will translate into caring. That caring will lead you to create a high-quality product, and people will respond to that because it is increasingly rare. While it may be easier to earn immediate returns from a business that is based on selling a dream, such as the multiple passive income schemes available from around the web, you will enjoy better, long-term earnings by providing a product that is valuable. This is because you will have satisfied customers who will continue to seek out and use your services.

There's another aspect here that will have a great impact on your earning potential: **time leveraging and referral marketing.** Referral marketing is when your company relies on, or pays for, word-of-mouth marketing. Your clients bring in more clients for you. This results in your product creating more revenue over shorter periods of time, essentially making your time more valuable. This is what time leveraging is. Both of these things will be covered in more detail later in this chapter, but for now, you should know that creating an excellent product is about more than providing a valuable service. It's also about ensuring your future financial security.

If you want to earn passive income, that's fine. The trick is to be certain that you are not becoming so passive in your business that you are no longer turning out a viable product. To ensure this, you have to **hire passionate people and**

treat them well. Only then can you walk away feeling confident that you will continue to provide a valuable service that continues to create reliable income.

Residual Income

The total sum of monthly earnings, for an individual or business, that are left over after all bills and expenses have been paid.

If you have residual income, then you're not living paycheck to paycheck. However, this doesn't mean that your income is passive either. Essentially, what it means is that you're earning enough money to cover all of your expenses while still having something left over at the end of the month. The money left over is your residual income. Obviously, this is not a type of revenue your business can earn so much as a designation for the earnings, so why have I included the definition here?

Many times, people lump residual and passive income together, making it sound as though they mean the same thing. This is why a definition is being offered here. If you find yourself on a website that lumps these terms together, find another source of information!

Make sure you're using good resources

You have to be discerning of what you're reading these days, especially considering what we discussed in the previous section. You can't automatically assume that what you're reading is accurate, and your best defense against inaccurate information is learning how to recognize it.

Wrong information is usually full of claims such as:

I'm an expert in my field

If a website or book continues to repeat and reinforce that the creator is a specialist, generally this is a sign that the product they're selling is a fancy marketing scheme dressed up as real information. An actual expert will likely not have to repeatedly tell you they are an expert because that will be obvious from the quality of their work. A real expert will also be able to offer a professional background to support their claims.

I know so many millionaires, and they all use this secret

The one "secret" millionaires use is sound business decisions based on accurate knowledge. You can bet your bottom dollar that a millionaire knows the difference between active and passive income, and they understand all the ins and outs of filing taxes and investing. Outside of winning the lottery, there's no quick and easy way to become a millionaire.

I got rich doing this, and so can you!

Sometimes this is true, sometimes the person writing those words has become wealthy and wants to teach you to do the same. However, at times this is a ploy to get you to buy into a program that doesn't offer valuable information. Learn to be discerning, and avoid get-rich-quick schemes at all costs

Above all, you should remember that anyone selling something that has no real value will still situate their information in some actual truth. Without an element of truth, chances are you wouldn't buy into what they're selling. Ironically, it is the smallest bit of truth that causes us to swallow the biggest lies. Be discerning, and know that anything worth doing takes effort.

Active Income

Income that is earned from employment, self-employment, investment dividends, and royalties. This income is often, but not always, reliant on the continued efforts of the earner.

Unlike passive income, active income is usually generated in proportion to the amount of time you spend working. If you currently work a nine-to-five, your weekly paycheck is active income. If you own your own business and actively work within it, you are earning active income. If you wrote a bunch of e-books and cash royalty checks every month, those checks are active income.

While, for the most part, active income is only earned if you're working; there are obviously forms of active income that can still provide revenue if you are not actively working.

Let's explores how this works using the example provided earlier of a jewelry-making business. Let's say you've reached that point where your business is generating passive income, but you still want to explore your passion for making amazing jewelry. You've reached a point where, after crafting jewelry on your own for so long, you've truly mastered the art.

Now it's time to use your mastery to redefine the field. Maybe you'll design a new type of clasp. Patent it. Then, every time another jewelry designer uses your clasp, you'll be earning royalty income. This is active income, but you don't have to put in much extra work once you've designed and patented the clasp. This adds active income to your passive income, and it keeps you engaged with your passion. It will lend further professional credence to you within your field, and it will increase the value of your jewelry by increasing the standing of your company within the marketplace.

Most likely, you will have to start out by earning active income. You can avoid this by hiring out the work right from the start, and this can even work for some passion-based businesses. However, while you're hiring out that work, you'll probably be earning active income from your day job. Rome wasn't built in a day, and your business won't be either. Through focused work and effort, you will get there!

Linear Income

Income that is earned as a direct result of an investment of time.

Unlike active income, linear income is specifically what you earn from spending time on a project. Your hourly job is both active and linear income. You royalty earnings are only active income.

Linear income is what most people are familiar with, and it is also how many small businesses stay small. A smart business person will understand that, if they consistently work within a mindset of linear income, they will always be doing business. Doesn't sound so bad, right?

Wrong.

Do you want to work until the day you die? Do you want to financially reset every month, making your bills in September, only to have to turn around and do it again in

October? Maybe you earn enough residual income to feel as though you're not starting from scratch every month. That's great; if it's also sufficient to pad a savings account for your retirement while also expanding your business.

If you're going to be successful truly, you have to find a way to move beyond forms of active and linear income and into forms of passive income with higher residual earnings.

So, now that you have a better understanding of what different types of income can be earned let's look at how to use this information to turn your passion into a viable and long-lasting business.

Turning your passion into a viable product

In the above sections, we covered a couple of basic examples that combine active and passive income to create a successful business. Now we're going to look at the various types of products you can create from your passion. First, we'll take a quick look at three basic types of products you can create; then we'll go a little more in-depth with each type.

By the end of this section, you should have a better idea of what kind of product you might like to make. Keep your personality factors in mind as you read about each product area. This will help you match your visualizations with the potential realities and come to a more informed decision.

There are three main types of products you can create from your passion:

- Information-based products: this refers to anything that sells a service instead of an actual physical product. This includes such endeavors as websites or e-books aimed primarily at teaching something or providing information.

- Craft-based products: this refers to a business that would provide an actual physical product. While an information-based business might sell DVDs, CDs, and books, the actual product is the information contained within. In a craft-based business, the physical product would be something such as jewelry, pillows, tools, or something else along those lines.

- Service-based products: this would be a business that provides a service such as ghostwriting, marketing, copyediting, and the like. The primary aim of this business is to provide services for other businesses and entrepreneurs.

Please note that the above designations were created for the use of this book. In general terms, the service industry refers to companies that work in retail and hospitality; information-based businesses usually operate within the world of Information Technology (computers), and a craft-based business would be considered manufacturing. The terms are being used differently in this book to provide a general idea of the different product areas in which you can apply your passions to create revenue.

To know what kind of product will be best for you, it has to align with both your passion and how you want to run your business. This means that you're going to have to pay attention to what you learned about yourself from Step 1, and what you learned about your passions from step 2. Keeping that in mind, let's get started.

Information-based products

An information-based product can take many forms:

- E-books
- Websites
- Learning programs
- Retreats and workshops
- Paid speaking opportunities

You are not limited to one product, but you will likely have to start narrow and work your way up. If you have a passion that involves sharing or spreading knowledge, then you may want to create an information-based product. This will require you to create a viable product from the information you want to share (let's say an e-book), then you will need to find a platform to sell your product (Amazon), and ways to market your work (Amazon reviews, social media, publishing articles related to your book and including a link to buy it at the end).

Now let's say your e-book has gained some traction, and you're ready to expand. You can write another e-book, and you probably want to start a related website if you haven't already done so. As part of this website, you can create a program that will offer a more hands-on approach to the information provided in your e-book. This program would consist of a series of videos you create that guide people through the process involved. They will use your website to sign up for and take this course.

Once this has become popular, you may want to offer weekend retreats where you—or a trained employee—takes the information even further and provides the client with an opportunity for real, hands-on learning. This also provides them with an opportunity to get to know you better, forming the feeling of a more personal relationship with your business and also promoting future customer loyalty and expansion. Once you gain a name for yourself, you may be able to find opportunities where you're now paid to speak on the subject for which you've been offering information.

Obviously, to get from the beginning to the end, you're going to need help. You can't fly around the country talking about your product if you're actively monitoring your website to ensure your market funnels are functioning properly. This is where it becomes important to know when and how you're going to transition from active to passive income. Is this going to be a gradual change, with you hiring employees as you go? Maybe you want to get to passive income a little sooner, in which case you would hire people from the start. This is entirely up to you and what you want your life to look like.

Let's go back to the personality factors that should weigh in your decision. If you're more of an active and extroverted person, you're probably going to be more comfortable hiring others to work with at the start. If you're more introverted and passive, you may want to work alone in the beginning. This is because an active and extroverted personality will thrive off the feedback they get from their employees, and they will thrive off of working with other people. A more passive and introverted person may not feel the same way. It may be easier for them to grow their ideas on their own for a little while longer before expanding to include others in the process of creation.

In fact, it may be tough for a highly passive person to engage in an information-based product at all because it will eventually require them to put themselves on stage. If you want to learn how to be less passive, this could be a good thing—but take it in stride. Don't push yourself so quickly that you quit because you become burned out or too scared to move forward.

This is why it's important to plan for your personal growth as you plan to grow your business. Maybe there are things you want to do, but you know you have to work your way up to being capable of doing them. That's okay; every successful person creates personal goals that align with their professional goals.

Craft-based products:

These take the form of anything you physically sell. You can combine a craft-based product with an information-based product if you want to, and many people use this to successfully grow their business over time.

The most important thing to consider when running a business that involves manufacturing is just that: manufacturing. As you grow, the demand for your product should (hopefully) grow. This means you will reach a point when you cannot successfully make everything on your own. You will likely need to hire out work sooner, and you are taking more of a risk by engaging in this kind of product creation.

If you find your greatest joy in the actual creation of the product, this could be problematic for you. Unless, of course, you create a high demand for something made by your hand. This is where you're going to have to become creative.

Let's say you are a painter. You can sell prints of your paintings for a small price, but the original for a much higher one. Maybe you are selling jewelry. You can have pieces that are mass-produced and sell for a low to medium price, and then you can have a separate line that sells for much higher prices because the products are hand-crafted by you or a highly-qualified/well-known artist. Maybe you can create a new process for what you're doing. Put a patent on it and either become the only person who offers that type of thing or enjoys the earnings from other companies paying to use your idea.

Then again, maybe you aren't selling something artistic at all. Maybe your product is more utilitarian. That can work out very well for you because you can just supply the design, or hire someone to make the design for you, and have the manufacturer produce the product. Of course, you are also going to have to figure out the distribution. Where will you sell your product? Can you make use of online platforms, eventually growing into putting your product on store shelves?

The answer is yes: there are many online platforms where you can sell your work. You can create your online store;

use sites such as Amazon, Ebay, and Etsy; or even start a campaign on a website like Kickstarter.

The main thing to keep in mind with this kind of business is that your expenses are going to grow significantly with your success. While this applies to any business, it is particularly the case when you are manufacturing goods. You need to keep this in mind when you're setting prices, hiring employees, and planning for the future.

Service-based products:

If you're offering service-based products, your income will likely become passive more quickly than with other types of products. This is because you'll be creating a business that seeks to provide services to other businesses.

Let's say you are running a business that delivers an information-based product. You don't want to do all of the writing yourself, so you find a company that will create content for your website. The company that creates your content is providing a service-based product. This company will likely have a staff of writers and editors whose job it is to create the high-quality content you expect.

If you're running a service-based business, you may start out as a freelancer. Over time, you realize that providing all the content for each client is too time-consuming. You're caught up in earning linear income because you only earn money when you're returning work for each customer. If you want to move out of linear income, creating higher levels of income each month, you might want to hire writers to work for you. This increases the amount of work you can deliver, and it ensures that you still have money coming in a while you're not working. As you grow over time, you will need to hire editors to check the work of your writers, a customer service team to respond to the needs of your clients, a marketing team to help you create new growth, a manager to oversee your employees, an accountant to handle your payroll and financial oversight, and so on.

Much like with a craft-based product, you are limited by the amount of work that you can feasibly provide as an individual when you offer a service-based product. This kind of work is dependent on the volume of return. In other words, the website you help to create will not be earning money for you—it will be earning money for your client. For you to earn a lot of money, you have to create a lot of content for a lot of different websites/customers.

Can't I combine all of these different types of products?

Yes, you can! If you sell a physical product, you can also run a website that teaches people about your process. You can even sell a program that teaches them how to recreate this process. This is turning your physical product into an information-based product, and it is one of many ways to grow your business.

Likewise, you can take your service-based product and use it to provide an actual physical or information-based product. Maybe you offer web-design as a service-based product, and you come up with a new program that makes web-design a cakewalk for anyone with a computer. That's a physical product you can now sell in addition to your service-based product.

You might feel as though you're undercutting your clientele base by offering something that does your job, but there are still going to be people who would rather outsource the work entirely. In fact, you could make the argument that it increases your client-base. There are always going to be people who would rather outsource the work, even if they can easily do it themselves. Now you've created a product you can sell to the people who would rather do it on their own, but might lack the technical skills required to accomplish this. You are only limited by your imagination and work ethic. Be creative and figure out what works for you.

The bottom line is that your product matters just as much as the need (or niche) you are trying to fill within the marketplace. You should consider the niche before you settle on the final form that your product will take.

What is your niche?

Within business, the term niche refers to a particular area of the marketplace that is catered to by a specific business.

Let's say you're writing an e-book about passive income. The e-book is the product; passive income is the niche. You need to consider if there is an interest or need for what you have to offer. Designing jewelry is great, but if your jewelry is the same as everything else available on Etsy, you're going to have a hard time staying competitive.

That's where we go back to quality. As was stated earlier in this chapter: quality can be its niche. There may be a thousand other products out there that offer the same thing as yours: that's okay, you just have to find a way to be better than those other products. Sadly, these days you can stay competitive simply by offering good quality. This is particularly the case for information-based products because it is easy to produce a low-quality information product and sell it with fancy marketing. Before the consumer realizes it, they've put money into something that wasn't worth the investment.

You want to avoid this, and here's why:

Breaking free from linear income means engaging in time leveraging and referral marketing.

This was covered earlier in the chapter, and now let's look at a more specific definition of each term.

Time-leveraging refers to the process by which you make your time more valuable as you grow your business.

Referral marketing is a means of using your clientele base to grow your clientele base.

When you are working from linear income, meaning that you can only earn money so long as you are actively engaged in the process of working, you can become caught up in just paying the bills. If you're smart, you'll look ahead to the future and find ways to grow beyond this.

That's where time-leveraging comes in. Successful use of time leveraging means that you are increasing the amount you can earn from the time you put into your business. To make sense of this, let's go back to the service-based product example from earlier.

When you were working as a freelancer, you only earned money every time you created and returned a product to your client. When you expanded your business by hiring people to do the writing for you, you turned every hour of writing into something much more profitable. You have successfully leveraged your time so that the total of hours worked by your employees will add up to exponentially greater profits for you. You are putting in less time, but earning more money. Time leveraging is a crucial component of earning passive income.

Effective time leveraging can be about more than higher financial earnings

The exciting thing about time leveraging is that, much like every other aspect of your business, it is only limited by your creativity and work ethic. Let's say that you're just starting out. You know what area you are passionate enough to work in, but you have a lot to learn before you can get to the place where money is rolling in with minimal effort. You can take classes, or you can find ways to get paid to learn the new skills you need to move forward.

For example, you've decided that you want to begin a website that teaches people how to become more spiritually aware. You know a lot about spirituality, but you don't' know anything about creating a website. You find a ton of websites that teach you how to do this, but it took you hours to compile enough valid resources to put together the knowledge that you need. Guess what; you've just discovered a need: readily available information about creating a website, written by someone who doesn't even know the basics.

Write an e-book about it and sell it on Amazon for a dollar. With effective marketing, over time you'll begin earning money that will pay for the time you had to spend learning about the topic. Writing the book will also ensure that you have a full understanding of the subject. This works because the best way to learn something effectively is to go about teaching it to others. This forces you to better organize your thoughts on the subject, to seek out more knowledge than you might have for yourself alone, and to ask more questions as you go. In the end, you'll know the subject much better and have created a product that will eventually provide financial returns for your time.

The message here is that effective time leveraging is about using your entire skill set to create money, and to build new skills. Your time is about more than just money; it's about the foundation you're laying for who you are going to become as you grow your business. If you only measure your returns in money, especially in the beginning, it will be hard to see where you're making real progress. It will be harder to bounce back from setbacks and failures because you may be overlooking where you've succeeded.

By putting out an e-book as you're building your website, you will also be creating a clientele base to work from. Perhaps you should use themes from your spiritually-based website in your e-book, and make sure to include a link to your site at the beginning and end of the book. Now you're not just earning money; you're creating clients for the other part of your business—making both more profitable! You're building an image for yourself in the marketplace, and you're increasing your credibility as a business person and thinker in your field. Maybe the people who love your e-book will tell their friends about it. You've just had your first experience with referral marketing!

Referral marketing is an essential aspect of the entire process if you want to be successful

An efficient use of referral marketing will create a self-feeding marketing machine that will continue to grow your business.

Referral marketing has been around for a while. Back in the day, it was known as word-of-mouth marketing. This is when your clients rave about you, and this brings in more customers. If you are creating a good and valuable product, this should happen naturally. However, you're still going to want to nurture the growth of your referral marketing.

You can do this by encouraging your clients to leave feedback, provide testimonials, or even by creating a system wherein your customers are offered discounts simply by referring friends and colleagues to your service. Over time, you will build a marketing machine that creates new customers while increasing the success of your business. By effectively combining this with time-leveraging you will continue to grow your earnings within your current market.

This will allow you the financial freedom and time to expand into other markets.

If you offer a bad product, on the other hand, you are undermining your ability to engage in referral marketing. Not only are you ensuring that the client you've brought in will not be coming back again, but you're also cutting off the potential to have them bring in more new clients. You might be successful for a while, but eventually, your business will fail.

If this is true, why do so many businesses offer bad products?

Because they're fly-by-night operations. These are the businesses that make the most outrageous claims about their products. These can be anything from 'lose ten pounds in a day!' to 'become a millionaire in a month!'. These companies are not seeking to offer anything of real value because they're actively preying on people's vulnerabilities. They don't have to worry about returning customers because, sadly, a desperate person will let go of their dollar far more easily than someone who feels more secure. While this will bring in clients for a while, eventually it will fail. This doesn't matter to the person running the business because they are probably actively engaged in their next fly-by-night scheme.

That's another reason why it's so important to know yourself well and to know why you're doing what you're doing. As a small business person, you're going to come across a lot of slick people looking to turn your dream into a quick dollar for themselves. Don't worry; you've got this. Just remember:

If you hear hooves, think horses, not unicorns.

Don't let your need to realize your dreams blind you to your gut instincts. If it feels wrong, doing it is probably wrong. If that marketing scheme your buying into sounds shady, it's probably shady. Learn how to trust your gut. Otherwise, you are not going to survive as a business. So, when someone tells you that you can quit your job tomorrow and move to a beach on Maui because you wrote an e-book, don't let your need for a vacation blind you to the reality of that statement. We all know this isn't possible, but most of us are overworked enough to believe it on our bad days. It only takes a minute to give your money to a false marketing ploy.

This goes back to the idea of positive outcome bias that was discussed in step 2. It is a natural human inclination to believe in the best possible outcome, and shady people will use this to make a quick buck. If you hear hooves and think unicorns, that means you're identifying with the best possible outcome and ignoring the reality. If you're thinking horses, then you're not allowing your circumstances to cloud your reality.

It's funny if you think about it because this means that reality is the true basis for logical positive thinking. If you buy into a false idea, this is only going to hurt you and your self-image. If, however, you set aside the stress and focus on the real possibilities, you will build your self-esteem as you enjoy positive results from sound decision-making. It's okay to ride atop your glorious unicorn steed, just remember that you are the one in control (not the fear-based, irrational part of your mind).

Referral marketing is about networking more than it's about selling

Creating a network means engaging with your customers and other businesses to build professional relationships. This can lead to new opportunities, to other businesses advertising your products, and to clients bringing in more customers.

We covered some methods for encouraging client-to-client referral marketing, now let's look at how to use your professional network to continue to expand this. We'll go back to the example of writing an e-book about web design. Another small business read your book and used it to revamp their web platform. They were so happy with the results, they contact you and let you know how much your book helped! Respond, and nurture this relationship. In your response, you should give a couple of insider tips you've learned since then—things that didn't appear in the book. Be friendly, and show them that continued interactions with you will create benefits for their business.

Once you've nurtured that relationship, find ways to promote each other using your websites. Now you've both put your products on new platforms, bringing in new clients using the reputation another business has earned with their customers. This is a priceless way to market as it won't cost you a dime—but you've expanded into a new or related market.

You can also work with other businesses to create unique products for your clients. Let's say you're spiritually-based website has some similarities to another site you've noticed. Instead of competing with this site, find a way to partner with them. Build a relationship, advertise for each other, and in the future create a product together that is available for a limited time through a shared website separate from your original sites. Both sites can advertise for this product, effectively introducing new clientele to each business. This will increase your visibility while building valuable relationships and solidifying your client's trust in your business.

Now that we've covered some general information about marketing let's switch gears and take a look at the process of switching from active to passive income. The next section will take a more step-by-step approach to taking your business from the beginning stages to passive income earnings.

Changing from active to passive income: knowing what role you will play in every step of the process

It's important to structure your business while keeping in mind what you want your life to look like. You have to know where you're going to make right decisions about how to get there. Assuming that you are starting from square one, meaning that you are in the beginning stages of your first business, the steps in this section will help you to plan better for your role in each stage of building your venture.

As with any journey, to get where you heading you have to:

1. **Know where you're going**

You've discovered your passion, and you know enough about your personality to know how to tailor your business to it. Now is the time to evaluate who you want to become, and how you want to fit the process of growing your business into your self-development. Now is the time to revisit your daydreaming. Not visualization. I'm talking about your biggest fantasies about what you want your life to look like. Imagine the wildest possibilities of what you could do, even if it seems impossible. Every impossible action that has ever been taken, from massive social movements to groundbreaking technological innovations, began as a dream. This isn't where you play it safe. Jump on your Unicorn and tell him you want to touch the stars! Fly wild, little warrior.

2. Come back down to Earth

As you spent time daydreaming, you should have been taking notes. Now it's time to review those notes and spend time visualizing. Imagine the day-to-day reality of what your wildest dreams would look like. Start at the end, then spend time ruminating on where you are now. From this process, you will put yourself in a better position to match your dreams with your reality because you will begin to see the practical steps that will get you from the beginning to the end.

It won't all happen at once, and you can't spend all of your time working things out in your head. Action, ultimately, is what creates a solid understanding of what steps to take. However, if you begin taking steps without thinking about where you want to go, you'll end up scattering your focus and burning out before you get anywhere. Know your intentions before you indeed start, then you will know what action to take next.

After that, you can

3. Begin researching potential markets for your business

You may already have a product in mind; that's great! Look for what is needed in the area of your business, and tailor your product to that. Find a gap, a need that isn't being fulfilled or adequately addressed, and then find a way to fit your product to that need. You can begin building business relations in this step. If you see a business that does something well, send them a message. Compliment them on what you see as their successes, and let them know you are getting started on your own business. Keep track of new contacts as you go, making notes in your address book about who they are and when you have had communications with each other.

Remember to keep in mind where you want to go, and what you want your life to look like as you get there. If you're already working 40 hours a week, you have to factor in how much time you have to feasibly research markets and develop a product. The good thing about having a day job is that you may have the money to hire out some of the work. While that's not taking a passive role, you are still going to be doing the work to get from that fancy marketing plan you bought to the result of selling a physical product; you will be able to streamline the process.

If you don't quite know what your product will be yet, that's great too! You can refine your ideas about what you want to sell as you look for lucrative markets. No matter where you are with your product, you should remember something important about markets:

A saturated market is not necessarily a bad thing

Most marketing companies would tell you to avoid an area where there is already a lot of competition. However, if there's a lot of competition; there's also a lot of interest. If you can find a way to exploit something new within a saturated market, you may just set yourself up too quickly create a large clientele base. As was discussed earlier, and throughout this book, quality can be its niche these days. Maybe you love working with people to help them discover their passion, but so many others are already offering such a program. Find a way to provide it in a new light, or using your particular process that no one else can match.

This is where knowing yourself well comes in handy. Remember when we talked about how your combined passions and interests create a unique identity? Use them to create a unique product within a saturated market. If it's indeed based on your interests and passions, people will not be able to copy you. They may try, but they will never deliver the same kind of product that you're providing because they are not you.

For example, we're all familiar with webcomics. There are tons of them out there, and some of them manage to become successful. Comics such as XKCD and The Oatmeal have become wildly popular. For every famous comic you see, there are probably another 100 that have come to nothing. What makes the difference?

The successful comic creators pander to a market that fits their passions and interests. It's probably a safe bet that making comics is something all of the people mentioned above feel passionately about, but these particular people have used their interests to create something truly unique.

XKCD uses a combination of humor, mathematics, and beautiful language to create content that you can't find anywhere else. Even without an understanding of mathematics, the creator manages to keep the content humorous and engaging. Many people have tried to copy

XKCD, with varying levels of success. It is the creator's obvious love of math, language, and drawing that sets the comic apart. No one can truly copy it because this person has effectively combined passion and interest to create something entirely unique.

The Oatmeal is the brainchild of Matthew Inman, and the comic plays on the internet's love of cats to draw readers in, and then Inman keeps them there with his wit and hilarious outlook on life.

Inman's story is quite inspirational. According to an article published by the National Wildlife Federation in May of 2013, an organization for which Inman has raised a lot of money, Inman was working as a programmer and website designer when he decided to supplement his income by creating a humorous dating website that included cartoons and blog posts. The site became so popular that Inman was able to sell it and pursue his love for creating comics as his full-time career.

Inman draws on his interest in bears and technology, among other things, to deliver content that is unmatchable as it is an expression of who he is. Others may try to copy it, but their work will never be as good because a copy is never up to the same standard as the original.

Now Inman has over 7 million readers. He has effectively used this platform to raise money for organizations and to support projects undertaken by friends. This is a prime example of how you really can turn your passions and interests into a viable business, becoming successful enough to support others in the same process.

So, when you're researching markets, don't always feel as though you have to avoid areas where there is saturation. People are always looking for something fresh and unique. If you can provide this, that saturated market may just be your golden opportunity.

Once you've found a valid market, on your own or with help, it's time to:

4. **Revisit your product**

Evaluate what you have to offer based on the markets you've found. Can you provide something new? Is there a need for what you're selling? Could you make small changes that would make your product even better? How many products can you offer within this area, and where should you start?

You can spend a little time daydreaming here. Start small and work your way up. Start with the most basic and simplest product you can produce, then graduate out into what you would sell if you had no limitations. Keep in mind what you imagined your life to be when you were daydreaming and visualizing.

Take notes on everything; this is the beginning of your ideas book. Keep it with you, and write down an idea for a product or a new market whenever they come to mind. Marketing and business are creative activities, and you never know when inspiration will strike.

Once you fully know what form you want your first product to take, and what kinds of products you would like to create in the future, it's time to:

5. Create a valid business plan

While we will cover all of the technical aspects of creating a business plan in the next chapter (Step 4), it is important to remember what role you want to play in your business as you're writing it.

Your plan will grow and change with your business. As we will see in the chapter on expansion (Step 5), your role in the company will change throughout your growth: not just when you reach the point where you want to switch from active to passive income.

So, while you're writing the plan for your business, you should keep your future and current goals in mind. If you're looking to take a passive role very quickly, you don't want to make plans to expand into a new market before you can afford to hire a decent marketing team or company. If you want to stay active, you shouldn't be allocating money to hire employees for work you can feasibly do on your own.

Your business plan not only sets out the core structure and mission of your business, but it also requires you to develop your marketing strategy and break down your product. This gives you an ideal opportunity to check your daydreaming against your visualization. Putting your plan on paper makes it more real, and this process will help you better understand when and how you decide to switch to passive income if you decide that's the route you want to take.

Deciding when it is time to switch from an active to a passive role

As has been discussed all throughout this book, when you switch from being active to passive is entirely up to you and the reality you want to create for your life.

So what do you want? Do you want to be a mogul? Do you want to focus on working with a close-knit group of people to create passionate products? Do you want to be able to take a six-month vacation, or to create enough residual income to support new businesses or altruistic endeavors?

What does your life look right now? Is the time you can put into your business limited more than the money you have to invest in it? Maybe your time and money are both limited, what then? Where are you now, and what do you want your future to look like?

These are the questions you need to ask yourself to figure out the point at which you're going to become passive in your business. As you're writing your plan in the next chapter, give some thought to each stage of the process. Your plan will include a marketing strategy and a financial plan, both of which will include projections for growth and earnings. It is from this reality, mixed with your abilities and goals that you should make your choice.

Let's say you've been creating webcomics like Mathew Inman. You're still working your day job, but your comics are starting to take off. Your inbox is filled with messages from fans, and haters, but you no longer have time to respond to all of them. You haven't given thought to how you're going to make money from this because, until now, you weren't thinking of it as a business.

You find a way to make money from your product. You put advertisements on your website; you begin to take endorsement deals and create web-comics about using products you love. You are now earning money from your comics, and you have the capital to expand. What about the time, though?

You see, it takes a lot of time to make a good webcomic. This is particularly the case now that some of your comics involve product-testing for your endorsement deals. You still can't handle the inflow of emails, some of which contain excellent opportunities for networking and growth. You're overwhelmed, but you're not ready to be passive either.

This is a crossroads point for your business. You have to pay attention to your choices here. If you decide to become passive, but find that you don't yet have enough revenue coming in to sustain hiring the employees this would take, you're going to run into a problem.

However, if you don't hire enough employees to handle the influx of work, you may become burned out and suffer a loss of clients because you falter in your delivery of the product. This will undermine your client-base, and that is never a good thing.

Maybe you aren't earning enough revenue to hire multiple employees, but you could afford a virtual assistant. This person would handle your emails, helping you to ignore the haters, respond to the fans, and sort through potential business deals.

Or, maybe you don't want to hire an assistant yet. You have another choice too. If you can afford an assistant, you may also be able to afford to quit your job. Then you can continue to work on your own, expanding until you can afford to hire more employees to work with you.

The choice you make depends on where you want your business to go, and where you want to go. If you quit your job, you will have ample time to handle your obligations, but you will also have less income. You might be able to expand your products more quickly by hiring an assistant and staying at your day job for a little while longer. You have to know if you can balance all of this in your life to find out what is right for you.

Let's say you hire that assistant and keep working. Your assistant totally streamlines your business, and you realize you have much more free time now. You begin to expand your products to include physical merchandise based on your comics. This goes well, so you take it a step further.

We're going to go back to The Oatmeal here to offer up an example of very creative product creation. Inman created a card game based on the Oatmeal comics. Something like that is so valuable because you not only have another product to sell, you have a product that creates a whole new level of referral marketing!

Imagine a customer bringing the card game to a friend's party. No one else there has ever heard of The Oatmeal, but everyone has a fantastic time playing the game. A portion of those people will buy the game and begin reading the comic, some will only purchase the game, and some will forget about it entirely. The point is, this product not only brings in revenue from sales, but it also brings in new customers.

Learn how to market your products

Stay creative with your product creation. Many times, earning more revenue depends on your ability to combine time leveraging and referral marketing. By creating a product that markets for you, you will enjoy increasingly higher returns on profits—at least for a while. This could put you in the position where you can truly quit your job. From this point, your choice to hire staff and take an increasingly passive role is determined by the reality of your earnings and the personal and professional goals you've set for yourself.

You are the only person who can decide when to become passive. Pay attention to your business. You have to have loyal and reliable employees who are united under the mission statement (core values and goals) of your business. Don't become passive until you know you can trust your staff to care as much as you do about your business. Don't go passive if you are actively enjoying being active in your business. Then again, you may want to become passive even if you're enjoying being active.

This is because you can take that energy and apply it to growing your business. I mean growing beyond new products and market. If you have successfully leveraged your time to be maximally valuable, you truly have the freedom for what comes next in your life.

You might want to start a new comic strip with all new characters, or find an entirely different business to create, or spend a few months in Hawaii. Just remember, too much relaxation is a bad thing. Besides, why to stop at one source of passive income earning when you could have two (or more).

You are only limited by your creativity and your work ethic!

Becoming wealthy means diversifying

Right now you might be asking yourself why you would want to run two businesses. After all, that seems like a lot of work for passive income.

Here's a little tip about how wealthy people become and stay wealthy: they have more than one source of income—whether active or passive.

Rich people run multiple businesses, make smart investments, and always have an eye to the future. Why not invest in a startup that correlates to your endeavor? You can market for each other. Every client they send you is another dollar in your pocket, and every customer you send them is also another dollar in your pocket because you invested in their business! That's how you use your money to make more money, that's how you leverage your time, and that's how you effectively use referral marketing.

So, if you're doing it right, you'll still be working. But you get to focus on the parts of the job that you love. Everyone else is handling the details: that's passive income. You can travel, take time off, start new endeavors. The world will be open to you, and you created that reality. Way to go Warrior! Give your unicorn an apple; he deserves it!

As you can see, it is your choice as to when and how you take a passive role in your business. Some people may prefer to work with the details longer than others. It's purely a personal decision. Make sure you do what feels right to you, and don't work yourself into burnout. Don't make the decision to keep an active role because you fear your business would fail if you weren't around to oversee every little thing. Instead, learn to trust yourself enough to feel confident that you've hired good people to work with you. Remember the advice from earlier chapters as well: hire passionate people and **treat them well**. A happy employee, who feels that they are cared about, will care more about the work they do. An employee who can pay their bills will be able to focus. An employee who isn't overworked will work harder and better. In short, be a good CEO, and you will have good employees.

Now that we've covered the basics of starting your business, we're going to get a little more technical. The next chapter, Step 4: Creating a business plan, will teach you how to officially organize your business. You will be provided with a standard template for a business plan, as well as guidance to help you turn that template into your personalized plan. A sample executive summary is included as well, but it is highly recommended that you find sample business plans online that fit specifically with what kind of business and products you will be creating.

Step 4: Creating a Business Plan

We've covered a lot of information so far, some that you may not even have realized would apply to starting a business—such as your personality. This is probably the most valuable chapter in this book, however, because your business plan will help you organize your business and keep you on track throughout the process of running it. You should revisit your plan as necessary, making changes to reflect what you've learned from doing business. You will also need a plan of activities if you intend to look for investors or loans to get started.

Business plans vary according to the exact nature of your business. However, some basic components should be present in every project. Those are what we will be looking at here. It is highly recommended that you search the internet for sample plans tailored to your particular type of business to ensure that you create a truly comprehensive document. The essential elements that every business plan should contain are as follows:

- Executive Summary
- Products and Services
- Market Analysis Summary
- Strategy and Implementation
- Company and Management Summary
- Financial Plan
- Appendix

These essential elements should appear in the order that they are presented above, but that does not mean you have to write them in this order. Also, please remember that your plan should be written with your needs in mind.

If you're writing with the intent to use your plan to garner investors, then you should pay attention to all of the particulars (such as including charts to represent financial data). If your plan is only meant to serve as guidance for you, then you can take some liberties with how much detail you decide to include. No matter what, your plan should be short and to-the-point. This isn't where you wax and wane philosophic, this is where you get down to business and lay out the facts, figures, and projections. No unicorns in your business plan, they won't be appreciated by potential investors.

Now that you have the general makeup of a business plan let's discuss each section in more detail. At the end of this explanation, I will provide a sample executive summary for a fictional business created for this book.

The sample will only include an overview because this offers a brief outline of all of the essential information in a full business plan. This will help you get started without overwhelming you with information. Your plan should be tailored to the type of business you are running and, as such, it is highly recommended that you find full samples of a business plan that fits your specific needs.

Executive Summary

This section should only total two pages, and it can be shorter. It acts as a summation of the key information from the rest of your plan, and some investors only want to see this portion to start with.

As such, it is critical that you present the most important elements of your plan using language that is easy to understand. Your executive summary should include the following sections in the order they are presented:

Value Proposition/Mission Statement

This is one sentence that should capture the main goal of your business. It comes directly from your business name and should leave the reader with an understanding of what makes your product or service valuable to the customer.

Problem

The idea of creating a compelling product or service revolves around solving a problem within a specific marketplace. In this instance, fulfilling a need is the same as solving a problem. This portion of the summary should highlight what problem or need you will be addressing with your products and services. For example, you notice that preschool teachers have a difficult time conveying information to clients at the end of the day. You have identified a need for a product or service that could make it easier for teachers to communicate with parents.

Solution

This section should address how your product or service will address the problem presented in the previous section. It is, essentially, an explanation of your product as regards the problem it solves. To continue from the above example, you determine that teachers would benefit from having paperwork that can be quickly filled out throughout the day. By selling different styles of these daily activity journals, you are adequately fulfilling the need/solving the problem presented above.

Target Market

This is where you present information about your targeted audience. The two key things to address here are:
Who is your target audience? You want to be specific here. Continuing with our example, "teachers" would not be a feasible answer. Preschool teachers are getting a little

closer, but you may want to narrow it down even further. "Preschool teachers from the United States who focus on education and social development in their programs" would be a good answer. The product you describe in your solution should be tailored to fit your audience.

Market Segments: This refers to potential buyers within your market. There is a commonly used way to identify and express this information, and it is as follows:

TAM/SAM/SOM:

TAM: Total Available Market—this is everyone you have the potential to sell to

SAM: Segmented Addressable Market—This narrows down the TAM, providing tighter focus for your marketing

SOM: Share of the Market—this is a realistic analysis of how many customers from your SAM totals that you can feasibly reach.

How big is your market base? This should be addressed using your TAM/SAM/SOM information. It is important to be realistic with your numbers. If you do not have a big enough market base, then you may need to re-address the need you are serving with your product.

Competition

Who is already attempting to solve the problem you've presented, and how are they doing so? How is your market base currently addressing this issue on their own? What gives you an advantage over the competition or qualifies you to serve better the problem you are addressing? You cannot leave this section blank or assert that there is no competition—every business will have someone or something to compete with.

Core Team and Employees

This section is critical, and some investors will pay more attention to this than to your product. Here you should describe your team and explain why they are fit to work on this project. What makes you and your team able to turn your idea into a product and successfully sell it within your market? Who are your key players and how are they going to contribute to your success?

Financial Summary

This should offer a summation of the critical elements of your financial plan. It's helpful to provide a visual representation, such as a pie chart or graph, that shows sales projections, expenses, and your potential profit earnings.

Required Funding

Do not make a pitch to potential investors here. This is simply where you state how much capital you need to get started.

Milestones

Here you will discuss future goals for your company as well as areas where you have already achieved a certain level of success.

That's it for the executive summary. If you do not intend to look for investors, you can skip this part of your business plan—or simply leave out sections eight and nine if you prefer to include it anyway. It may be a good idea to write an executive summary simply to have two pages that give a brief overview of the critical parts of your plan. This will help you stay focused, and help you to make changes as you go. It is also a valuable resource for your key employees as it will ensure everyone within the company is on the same page about your ultimate goals. Now we will move on to the next section.

Products and Services

Remember the problem and solution sections of your executive summary? This is where you will expand on those sections, and it is a vitally important part of your plan. You should start by describing the problem or need you are addressing in detail, explaining exactly why it is a problem. After this, you should describe your product or service. Then you should carefully explain how your product offers a valid solution to the problem you presented.

While there may not be room for unicorns in your business plan, horses are always welcome. NEIGH!

It is not good enough to only sit around and think about what need you might address. Ideas exist within the ephemeral realm of the unicorns. To ground your ideas in reality, sometimes, you have to do actual footwork. Early thinkers thought the Sun revolved around the Earth (which was obviously flat, duh) because they never bothered to test their theories. Man, *were they wrong*!

The same is true for your business. If you're uncertain about your problem or solution, then go out and ask! Find someone who might be a potential client, confirm that they experience the problem you are trying to solve, then pitch your product to them. Do this with as many people as you feasibly can, process their feedback, and use that information to fine-tune your problem and solution.

Market Analysis Summary

This is where you'll offer the details as regards your targeted audience (a.k.a your market), their needs, trends within the market, the potential for growth within the market, key customers (those who would greatly benefit from and be a benefit to your business), expansion into future markets, competition, and your advantages over the competition. The information should be broken into different sections, and you can use the sample business plan provided at the end of this chapter to see how this should be done.

Strategy and Implementation

This section should offer specifics as to how you plan to proceed. It will include a marketing and sales plan, as well as sections which detail the specifics of how your business will run. This includes your location; what equipment, and tools you will need; and the major goals or milestones of your business. Let's take a quick look at what your marketing and sales plan should include:

Positioning: This is how you present your product on the marketplace. What is your gimmick? How are you addressing your audience based on their needs, and how does it set you apart from your competitors? This does not need to be very long, but it should adequately explain what makes you stand out from your competitors.

Pricing: Your pricing should correlate with your positioning within the market. You need to take your costs into account while also being appropriate for your target audience. High prices will cost you, customers, while low prices may devalue your product in the marketplace. You can determine your pricing by your costs or by the value your client would assign to the service you are offering. Either way, your costs should be factored into your price.

Promotion: This is how you plan to communicate with your customers about your product. It can include packaging design for a physical product, advertising strategy, and how you plan to reach customers through means that don't directly sell. This includes media coverage of your business and the use of content that offers valid and useful information to your market base with the direct intent to improve your company's value to potential clients, and the indirect intent to convert readers into new customers. You should also include social media strategies here as these are becoming essential to running a business.

Partnerships: This is only important if you have already formed a partnership with another business, or if you plan to. A partnership should benefit both companies, with each organization providing something of value to the other.

Business Summary

This section is only essential if you will be using your business plan to attract investors. You may want to include it anyway, even if you're not looking for investors, as it will help you organize your thoughts about the basic structure of your business. It will likely be one of the shortest sections of your plan. It should begin with a mission statement that aligns with your value proposition. Keep this statement short, less than a paragraph.

After the mission statement, you should describe the legal structure of your business. Are you going to be a Limited Liability Company? Sole Proprietorship? C – Corp, S – Corp, or Partnership? Are you the sole owner of the business, or have you split ownership between partners?

Next, you'll want to give a brief history of your company, no more than a few paragraphs. This should include notable successes and be situated within the information from the rest of your plan.

The last thing you should address in this section is your primary headquarters, as well as any satellite locations from which you conduct business.

Financial Plan

While this section of your plan may be the one you dread most, it is also crucial. You can't conduct effective business if you don't understand the flow of money through your organization. Usually, the fear of completing this portion is worse than the actual thought and work it takes to do it.

Your financial plan should offer monthly projections for the first year of earnings, and yearly projections for the next three to five years. After this, you should detail your sales forecast. Basically, for this, you will give a projection for intended sales of each product or service that you offer. Every product projection should be immediately followed by the cost of that product (this means the specific expense entailed in creating that specific product).

This section of your plan should focus more on projections and less on past earnings. You can and should include past earnings if they are pertinent to your future projections. If so, your financial plan should include a **profit and loss statement**. This is where you put all of your costs and earnings together to show if you are making a profit or not. It is essential to keep track of this as you do business, and you should be creating quarterly profit and loss statements to keep track of whether or not your strategies are effective.

You can find a lot of detailed information on the web which will guide you through how to create a healthy profit and loss statement. There are also programs that can do this for you, such as Quickbooks Pro. These programs can be expensive, but they're worth it because you simply have to plug in various information and the program will produce a valid statement.

Another key element to your financial plan is the **cash flow Statement**. While profit and loss keep track of where you are earning or losing money, your cash flow statement will keep track of fluctuations in the liquid cash that is immediately available to your company. When you make a sale, that is immediately included in your profit and loss statement. However, it is not included in your cash flow statement until the client has paid for the product or service.

Next up is your **balance sheet**. This is a quick overview of your company's financial standing. It will include your assets and liabilities, and your equity. The net worth of your business is calculated by subtracting your liabilities from your assets.

The final section to include in your financial plan is your **exit strategy**. No, this isn't what you plan to do if you fail. It's the exact opposite! This is what you will ultimately do with your company once you reach the end of your journey and look towards new horizons. Are you going to sell your business to another company and, if so, are there any potential buyers that you are already aware of? Investors will want to know this information, especially considering that their return usually comes in when the company is sold.

Speaking of investors, if you have them, your financial plan should also include a section detailing how you plan to use the money they've invested in your company. This should come in before the exit strategy, and it should provide an overview of the main ways in which their money will be used. It should be as brief as possible.

Appendix

This section is only necessary if you have notes, industry-specific definitions, charts, graphs, patents, product design illustrations, or any other information that doesn't fit neatly into the rest of your plan. The reason you want to include information such as this in the appendix instead of in the body of your plan is simple: you want to make it as easy as possible for the person reading your plan to understand it. If the information is valuable, but not essential, it should be included here so as to keep the body of your method as short as possible.

As promised at the beginning of this chapter, now we're going to take this information and apply it to a fictional executive summary created for this book. I feel like we need a little break from all this serious, technical writing; so our sample executive summary will be from a clown college in southern Nebraska. As you read through this plan, you will notice that certain parts of it have been **emboldened**. This is because these areas of the sample are problematic. After the sample, I will go through these elements and explain exactly why they are not sufficient for the summary.

1. Executive Summary

Maxwell's Prestigious Clowning Institute

1.1 Value Proposition:

Our company provides serious services for unemployed individuals seeking to turn their wayward lives into a viable, traveling clown show. We offer various programs that, upon successful completion, will provide the foundation for un or under-employed individuals to create, license, and implement their act.

1.2 Problem

In today's tough economic climate, many people find themselves without enough income to support their lifestyle or that of their family. In such dire times, the demand for both **alcohol** and entertainment rise.

1.3 Solution

Our services will train individuals in an area that provides them with a proper foundation to achieve financial success, therein solving their unemployment problem. At the same time, this person is now in a position to provide a valuable need created by the harsh economic environment: entertainment. **While they may also provide alcohol, that is up to them.**

1.4 Target Market

1.4.1 Total Available Market (TAM): With national unemployment at 25% (one-quarter of the entire population of the United States), our TAM is estimated at 79,725,000 people.

1.4.2 Segmented Addressable Market (SAM): Our focus is on male and female individuals who are between the ages of 20 and 30. This comprises roughly 40% of the total of unemployed individuals, making our SAM 31,890,000 individuals.

1.4.3 **Given the increasing popularity of clowns due to a recent re-emergence of popular iconic figures such as Bozo and Ronald McDonald**, we expect to immediately take advantage of 3% of our SAM. This calculation represents the increasing interest in clowning, as well as the particular faction of unemployed individuals, within the appropriate age range, **who also enjoy traveling**. As such, our SOM number is 956,700.

1.4.4 Our current projections of our total market base are approximately **1 million individuals**.

1.5 Competition

Our main competition is Curly-Wigs Clowning College and Bistro. Curly-Wigs offers a state-of-the-art facility that covers every aspect of clowning, from squeaky noses to squeaky shoes. They currently provide work-study programs, through employment at their on-campus bistro that is open to the public, which helps lower the cost of their program for students. However, even with decreased cost, Curly-wigs is still an expensive institution that only offers on-site training. Their focus is on stationary acts and not those of the traveling circus variety. Maxwell's provides a more cost-effective program which can provide in-person training at our facility, or distance-training through our many online programs. In short, we offer lower prices during troubling economic times and more options for how and when a student can take a course.

1.6 Team

Maxwell Filibuster Quick wickets III is the owner of Maxwell's Prestigious Clowning Institute. Maxwell is a third generation clown who has worked within the industry most of his life. Our core team includes web-designer Patricia Milligan, who specializes in creating online tutorials; Humor writer Harry Pear, who can create amazing content for our online courses and advertising needs; and Sylvia Plinth, an award-winning educator who will oversee the creation of our curriculum as well as our teaching staff. Together, this team will be able to create engaging content, draw clients to our services with the surprising and humorous advertisement, and create courses that truly serves the needs of our customers.

1.7 Financial Summary

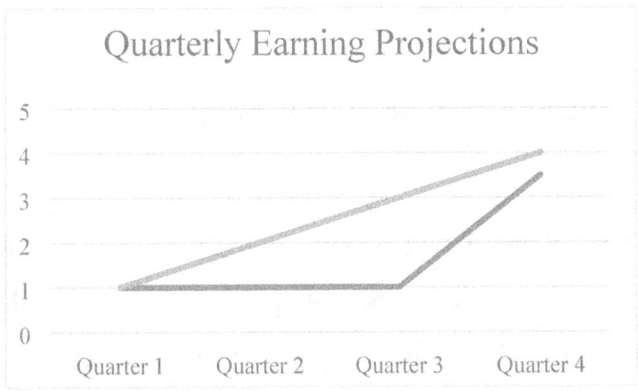

1.8 Required Funding

It is estimated that Maxwell's will require $75,000 in capital to get started.

1.9 Milestones

Maxwell Filibuster Quick wickets III has a reputation for being the funniest and most well-loved clown in the history of the United States. His reputation has already garnered interest from over 2,000 potential students, and it is this interest that inspired Maxwell's Prestigious Clowning Institute. We aim to train and license **10,000 new clowns**.

Okay, as you can see from the above, it's not that scary to get started on your business plan. Now let's take a look at the emboldened portions of the above sample and see where Maxwell made some mistakes.

Don't include extraneous information

In the problem section of his summary, Maxwell includes something that he does not plan to address: alcohol consumption. His business in no way provides this service, yet he mentions it twice. Your plan should not contain extraneous information, and it certainly should not discuss products and needs that you will NOT be addressing.

Make sure your reasoning is sound

Maxwell asserts that the rise in popularity of iconic clowns is why his clowning school will be effective. However, does the popularity of iconic clowns necessitate an increase in the demand for traveling clown shows? An icon tends to play on people's sense of nostalgia—something that may not translate into an interest in a living, traveling clown show. In the same vein, a rise in the demand for entertainment is too general to be a valid reason for opening a clown school. Is there research that shows what forms of entertainment tend to rise with unemployment?

That's the information that should be included here, and only if it supports the creation of your business. As such, the logic upon which Maxwell has structured core elements of his plan is faulty. While people may demand more entertainment, they may not care about clowns. While clowns are becoming popular again, this trend may not last, and it may not equate to more people wanting to pursue clowning as a profession.

A huge market base is not necessarily a good thing

The next issue is that Maxwell's potential market base of 1,000,000 individuals is far too large! It probably wouldn't even be possible for Maxwell to adequately serve all of these customers, even with offering online courses as an alternative to on-site training. This problem has arisen because Maxwell has not effectively narrowed down his base. He aims to bring in unemployed clients between the ages of 20 and 30 who like to travel.

However, enjoying traveling does not mean that one would like to make a career of it. Instead, it might be better for Maxwell to look at individuals who have expressed a direct interest in traveling for their careers. This would represent an even smaller number. While it may seem like a good idea to have the biggest number possible here, that shows that your business is not focusing tightly enough on one market segment to adequately advertise and turn potential clients into real customers. You cannot please everyone, nor should you try to.

Your financial summary should be realistic

There are several problems with the above financial summary. To start with, the graph doesn't include enough information for the reader to fully understand it. There's no information that lets the reader know if the numbers are expressed in thousands, hundreds of thousands, or what. There is also nothing that lets the reader know if this is projected sales regarding units of products moved or the profit made from moving products.

The graph itself is also unrealistic. Many businesses make the mistake of projecting flat earnings until they get to a turning point where sales take off. This creates the kind of graph used in the above example. While this is a common mistake, it is entirely unrealistic. True projected earnings will not follow such a pattern, and potential investors will know that you haven't done your homework if this is the kind of projection you create for them.

The last thing that's wrong with this section is that it should include more than a graph. The graph should be explained, and there should also be accompanying charts that give a three-year projection for how many units of product you plan to move, the cost of creating the product per unit, the price at which each until will be sold, and the projected gross (total earnings from the sale of goods) and net income (your income after all costs and expenses have been paid) for the number of units you plan to move within the next three years.

Make sure your team accounts for all of your core needs

At first glance, it may seem like Maxwell has done a good job in describing his team. However, he has left out a few key people. His team should probably include someone who works within finance, and someone who has experience in marketing. While it's great to have a good writer to help with your advertising, the market strategy is a different game entirely. The whole purpose of your team is to prove to potential investors that you can effectively bring your product to market and sell it for a profit. You can't do this if you don't know how to evaluate your cash flow or market your product.

Make sure your goals are fully expressed

Finally, Maxwell's milestone of 10,000 new licensed clowns is not quite accurate enough. To make this a valid milestone, Maxwell will have to include a relevant timeframe for the successful licensure of these 10,000 traveling clowns. A goal or milestone should include what you aim to accomplish within a specific timeframe.

As you can see, a lot of critical thought should go into your plan. This is why it's so crucial to use samples that are tailored to the kind of business you will be running. Avoid extraneous information, but make sure that you include the necessary basics to provide a solid overview of your operation.

Honestly, it would take an entire book to explain all the ins and outs of writing a good business plan. There's a lot to learn here, and that's why I've only covered the basics. It is your responsibility to continue to research and tailor your business plan as you go. You can do personal research, take a course, or join a professional network to pick up the skills you need in this area.

You should aim to improve the plan every time you make changes to it. Allow yourself the room to make mistakes. After all, mistakes can teach us the best lessons if we approach them with the right mindset.

That's it for Step 4!

In the next step, we'll look at some traditional and creative ways to expand your business once you've grown beyond the beginning stages. The final chapter will offer a summary of the most important information to remember from this book.

Step 5: Intelligent Expansion

The expansion is exciting no matter what form it takes. This is because being able to expand your business means that you are successfully managing your affairs. Your plans are bearing fruit, and you have reached that point where you get to take things to the next level.

There are many different points at which you can expand and different ways in which you can do so. At the beginning of your endeavor, expansion may only mean growing to include more markets. It can also include creating partnerships, extending the range of products and services that you provide, creating strategies to handle an increasing demand for your products, or even starting a new endeavor once you've reached the point of passive earnings.

While this is an exciting time for your company, it can also be a dangerous one. If you expand too quickly, or not fast enough, you may hurt your profit margins. As such, it's important to know how and when to expand. This will depend on what you as an individual want, what is good for your company and your employees (if you have any), what opportunities for growth are currently available, and—above all—what foundation you have laid to support expansion.

The reason you have to take all of the above into account is that expanding is going to change your business. Depending on the nature of expansion, these changes can be either small or drastic. An example of a small change would be your company deciding that it's time to change marketing tactics by offering click-link information articles about your industry. These materials primarily serve as a source of information, but they are written with the intent to increase your existing customer's trust in the company while also encouraging potential customers to become new customers.

My business is doing great, and I'm ready to make massive changes!

Hold up there, cowboy! You don't want to let your unicorn run away with you. Significant changes are great because they show that you have indeed broken through to the next level of business. However, if you change too much and too quickly you are risking your business. The most dangerous thing you could do is make changes simply for the sake of making changes. Take a look at the following example to see exactly what I mean.

Let's say your business has, to this point, been a sole proprietorship. However, you've come to a place where you know you can no longer handle the demand for your product alone. For this example, you're offering an information product that takes the form of web tutorials that teach older generations how to use new media. Your clients love your work, and your inbox is flooded with emails you just don't have the time to respond to. The ones you have read show that there is an increasing demand for tutorials that approach areas for which you do not have the knowledge to teach adequately.

You now need teachers with a particular skill set that can create video courses for your website, a financial advisor to help you track your profit and loss and cash flow, video editors to polish the content created by your teachers—and possibly to record it, an assistant to handle incoming client emails, and perhaps a manager to oversee everyone.

Determine your growth by the foundation you have already set

It is your success that has created more of a demand for your product, as well as a demand for new products. Most likely your clients are talking about you to their friends, and referral marketing has created a lot of the growth that you're seeing. This means that you probably don't need to hire a marketer as your business is already growing. You're going to be spending a lot of money to hire the people you need to sustain your current workload. You might consider hiring someone to create new marketing strategies in the future, but if you do so now, you risk creating more growth at a time when you are already feeling strained by your client load. This is how you grow according to the foundation you have set: make smart decisions about what you need, and know when to slow or maintain your growth according to what future demands it will place on your business.

So, instead of continuing to expand your client-base, in the above example, you would seek to expand your employee-base and possibly restructure your business. Perhaps it's time to move from being a sole proprietorship to a limited liability company. This will involve including other people to act as officers in your business, meaning that the way you operate within your organization is going to change. While this will have benefits, it will also have drawbacks. Either way, it means a new way of doing business for you. There will be a learning curve.

Hiring more employees, or your first employees will also change the dynamic within your workplace. You'll have to figure out how and when you're going to train everyone, or if you need to hire an outside company to provide training. You will have to address workman's comp, payroll, PTO and sick days, benefits, and all of the other things that come with having a staff. You need to determine how many new teachers you'll need, or if you'd rather hire a writer and continue to record all of the content on your own. To make this decision, you need to have realistic projections as to potential future earnings based on your present situation. This way, you will know how many new employees you can feasibly hire, or if you would be better served by hiring freelance writers, programmers, and web designers to design new courses for you.

Proper growth is essential to achieving passive income

As you can see, growth should never be taken lightly. It is an exciting time for your business, but it should be approached with intelligent thought, foresight, and caution. Otherwise, you risk making a critical error that could cost you the business you have worked so hard to establish. If you play your cards right at this crucial juncture, this may be your last big push before you get to the point of passive income earnings.

If you fail at this stage, pick yourself up, dust yourself off, and start again. Learn from the failure, and move forward. Make sure you look at where you went wrong and do some research to establish what you could have done to avoid this situation. Next time around, you will be sure to steer clear of the mistake.

The above is an example of internal growth that changes the structure of your organization, but what about other types of growth? We're going to take a look at three more ways in which you may experience expansion, and how to handle it when the time comes to make changes indeed. The first is growing your products and services, the second will look at the kind of growth that is possible when you've taken a passive role in your company, and the final example is expanding into investing in or acquiring other businesses.

Expanding your products and services

In Step 3 we discussed different options for the types of products that you can offer for your business. Expanding your products and services can take two primary forms:

- Broadening the number of products or services you sell within the current framework of what your company offers, effectively reaching more people within your target market.
- Expanding the scope of the products and services that you offer, effectively tapping into new markets.

The first type of product expansion is a smaller version of growth than the second. If you're manufacturing physical products, it may entail hiring more employees for your manufacturing and distribution. If you're doing a lot of business, you may even need to expand your manufacturing capacity by opening new factories and hiring the employees to fill them.

Obviously, this has to be done carefully. You must ensure that your balance sheet balances, meaning that you have to know if you will earn enough from selling more products to make up for the increased cost of having additional manufacturing facilities and employees.

If you're not manufacturing a physical product, there are still ways to expand your products and services within the framework of what you're already offering. If you're making webcomics, maybe you decide that you want to experiment with new characters. Every character carries the potential to be its merchandising gold mine, so this may not be a bad idea. This would only be considered expanding into a new market if you were writing for a different target audience. If your audience remains the same, then you are only building off of your first endeavor. If you sell e-books, consider looking at different topics to write about that would still hold interest within your base market. If you sell a service, such as running an e-book publishing company, expanding your products and services within your current market would entail something such as finding new writers to cover topics that are already of interest to your current market base.

These are smaller and safer methods of growth, but what about when you're ready for something bigger? If you've already grown as big as your current market will allow, and you have the net profit and cash flow to do so with minimal risks, then it's time to expand into new markets.

You can do this by offering similar products in a new way. For example, an e-book author could begin to write books on subjects that cater to a market segment that is related to but separate from their base market. This would entail some risk as there is no guarantee that your new books will sell well enough to ensure an adequate return on the time it took you to write them. By now, however, you should have become better at gauging and responding to the needs of various markets. As such, so long as you act within the parameters of your common sense and good judgment, you will minimize your risk.

If you offer a physical product, such as T-shirts, expanding a market would entail selling a different style of shirt that caters to a different audience. It could also include manufacturing other types of clothing to go with your t-shirts.

Let's say you've been selling t-shirts that cater to a pre-teen demographic. You've been in business for a few years, and the pre-teens who loved your shirts are now teenagers. You have a golden opportunity here to tap into a new demographic: teenagers. The pre-teens who loved your old shirts will also likely love your new shirts simply because they are already familiar with the brand. This may lead to referral marketing; wherein your now-teenaged customers are encouraging their friends to wear your t-shirts. Or, they may inspire younger customers to buy from your original line as they seek to impress their older friends.

The best way to expand is to ensure that your new market segment or demographic relates to your core audience in some way. It wouldn't make sense if, like a t-shirt manufacturer, you suddenly began selling pocket watches. Not only would you have to deal with a different kind of manufacturing, but you would also be starting from scratch with your marketing.

The other way to expand your products and services is to offer a different type of product than you usually offer. Much like with the t-shirt example above, your new product should correlate to your old ones. A good illustration of this was provided in an earlier chapter when we discussed Matthew Inman of The Oatmeal. He started out making comics, and eventually he offered merchandise (including a card game) that featured characters from those products. This is a type of product expansion that utilizes your current market base and, especially considering the example offered by Inman, may even be able to help you expand it. As people use your mugs or play your game with others, they will be advertising for you—and they paid you to do it instead of the other way around!

You can also offer new products that are geared towards a different market segment. Let's go back to the example of a company that provides web-tutorials teaching older generations how to use new media. Let's say you've got all you can handle regarding this kind of instruction. Now it's time to see who else might have a technical question in this area that needs answering. Is there a market for videos that teach people how to use different social media sites for marketing? Exploit it and, while you're doing so, attempt to convert your existing clientele into customers for your new courses as well. Maybe some of them were studying how to use new media so they could use it for their business! Now you've expanded into a new market while also catering to your previous market segment.

The main thing to take from the above example is that you cannot ignore or under-served one market segment only because you are looking to expand into another. It will do you no good if your growth in one area causes you to shrink in another. That's why you have to maintain oversight of any endeavors to expand your business.

Isn't this supposed to be a book about passive income? Why do you keep telling me to work?!

You can't get too passive income without understanding how to start and grow a business. As has been mentioned throughout this book, while the rewards are worth it, you're going to have a lot of work to do before you can slide into a passive role. To keep yourself motivated, you need to learn to recognize your achievements as you go. Growth is a mark of achievement and success. You will probably need to expand your business once or twice before you reach passive income. At that point, expansion will become something you simply have to oversee. Your employees will handle the details.

Most people who love what they do have a hard time taking a back seat in their business. Unless of course, it means they can spend more time doing what they truly love. This is where we get to expansion in the passive role. This does not include the expansion that is being handled by employees in your business. This is your expansion. Your growth. This is what you're going to do now that you've reached the point of passive income.

Are you going to find another passion and start another business? It's not a bad idea, having more than one source of passive income. This will increase the amount of work you have to do as you'll now be playing a passive role in two companies, but you'll also be earning twice as much.

If you do decide to start another business, you have nearly an infinite number of possibilities open to you. You will have more capital than you did when starting your first business, you will have a better reputation—putting you in a better position to attract investors, and you will have a much better idea of what to do to get started. The world will be your oyster, and it's because of all the hard work you did to get here.

If you don't want to start another business, consider looking for new ventures to purchase and merge with your own.

If you do this, you want to focus on organizations that will help your business. Buy out the competition and combine their clientele with yours. If you can't buy out the competition, negotiate a partnership in which both companies would benefit.

You see this every day. Whenever T-mobile runs a commercial denouncing Verizon, they are advertising for the other company. It may appear like they're attempting to undermine the competition, but this is another form of advertisement that businesses use—and it is one way that large companies within the same industry support each other, even if it looks like competition on the surface.

Let's say you're earning passive income from a business that specializes in giving golf tutorials. One day, you're playing on the green when you just happen to run into the CEO of a company that produces luxury, high-end golfing equipment. Wine and dine them, discuss working with them, and see if you can create a partnership in which your companies advertise for each other. Maybe you could go a step further, perhaps you could work it out so that your clients get a discount when they shop with the other company, and maybe the other company could offer a deal where buying an individual product comes with a discount for your services.

Of course, you don't have to have a partnership to do this. Let's go back to the option of buying. What if you buy out the company that manufactures the high-end golfing equipment? Now you can funnel clients between your businesses, use your businesses to advertise for each other, and effectively drive expansion between the two.

This brings me to another form of expansion: vertical integration. This refers to when one company offers complementary products and services that would typically be provided by two different companies. Ideally, some of the products would be involved in the manufacturing of the other products. So, if you're selling chairs, you might want to buy the company that supplies the wood your chairs are made from. Now you have effectively cut costs for manufacturing your chairs while also opening up a new way to make money: selling the wood to other companies while also using it to make your chairs.

The entire point of reaching passive income is that it allows you to grow far beyond active and linear income. You can now fully take advantage of time leveraging because you will have the financial freedom and time to think immense. If you have knowledgeable employees who care about your business as much as you, then you can make it their job to find new avenues for expansion on its largest scale. While you will have to oversee the process, and possibly be present for the complex negotiations, you can leave the details and hard work to your executives.

Expansion means that your role within the company has to change

After your first true expansion—the one that changes the structure of your business, you should not be taking as much of a hands-on role. This is because you're going to be needed elsewhere. There are some common problems that arise when big growth occurs in business, especially when this marks a shift from a small business to a larger company. For a while, your job is going to be seeing your business through the major changes that come with growth. Some of the common problems you may have to deal with include:

Maintaining the founding ideals of the company

It is easy for a company to adhere to it foundational principles when it has ten employees, but what about when it has 1,000? Someone has to be staying on top of how you do business. While you can eventually hire executives to do this for you, to start with you, want to keep your eye on how the way your employees operate is changing. You have to nurture this growth the same way you nurture your inner growth: allow room for the changes that need to occur but make sure they are in alignment with the core values of what you want your company to be. This will ensure that you don't lose a lot of clientele while you're restructuring because they feel their trust has been broken by your company's changes.

Changing infrastructure and resultant needs

As your company grows, you're going to need to revisit how you keep financial records and how you make projections. This may involve hiring even more staff, such as a team of accountants and financial advisors.

Additionally, the roles of some of your employees will change while you also may need to make room for new positions. It is imperative to ensure that you are not growing so quickly that your need for more employees overshadows your increased earnings. There is no point in growing if it will not eventually result in a wider profit margin.

Disagreements among your core operating staff

Remember your team, the one from your business plan. It's easy to get along with your team when your company is small, and the decisions you have to make are limited. However, as you grow, this will change. Your business has to change, and that is inevitably going to cause discord.

Customer Service

Having more clients means you're going to need people who can filter and respond to their questions and concerns. You can't please everyone all the time, so people are going to have issues. The more people you sell to, the more people will complain. If you don't want to lose clients, you're going to have to create an excellent customer service department and ensure it has adequate staff to meet your demands. Excellent customer service is essential to your referral marketing and future growth, so you cannot ignore this aspect of your business.

Personnel Changes

Some employees will see the increase as an exciting opportunity to move up in the company; others will see it as a threat to what they want their work environment to look like. You are going to lose some staff, but you will keep some too. Be prepared to say goodbye to people who have been with you since the beginning. Don't hold it against them; everyone is entitled to choose what they want their life to be like.

You're going to need more capital

With more staff to hire, some employees leaving, other employees being promoted, an increased cost of production, and the myriad other things that will cost you money; you're going to need plenty of capital to make the necessary adjustments required by growth. That's why it's so important to make sure you're ready for it. While increasing demand from your customers may make it seem like a good time, if you don't have the cash to back up the changes you will fail. This may be a time when you take on an investor. Remember, an investor makes their money back when you sell your company. They are going to want to know your plans for doing so, and if you don't have any, you probably won't get an investor as they will likely never see a return on their investment.

As you can tell, the passive role is not so passive. It still takes work. This is why some people choose to stay small. They choose not to expand, and that is an entirely valid option. If you can keep your business running, creating enough profit to live comfortably, then major growth is not a requirement.

That's why, in the introduction to this book, I stated that it's not wise to seek out passive income as a means of creating more time for your family or an extended vacation. It's going to be a while before you can become truly passive. Additionally, anytime your company expands you are going to be temporarily stepping into an active role. You will have control over when and how this happens, but it's still going to take time and effort to continue to grow your business.

Conclusion

If earning passive income is so much freaking work, why do people do it?

Why do people do anything?

Because we can.

Don't do this if you want to be lazy. Do it because you saw a genuine need in society, and you have a passion for addressing that need through your business.

It can be anything. It can be your hobby, your area of expertise, a valuable service. It could be an altruistic endeavor aimed at truly improving some broken aspect of humanity.

Do it because you love it. Do it because thinking about it makes you swell up with excitement on the inside. This path is going to test you in every way possible. You will grow tremendously throughout the process. To create a passive income business, you have to want it. You have to be willing to make sacrifices for it. And that's the best reason to build a business:

It will make you a better person.

Anything worth doing is worth it because it improves you. By improving yourself, you will improve the world around you (so long as you are going about your business ethically).

And that's why you have to know who you are before you start. Know who you are, and who you want to be. Only then can you decide if the effort is worth the reward.

And, as you and your unicorn prance merrily down the path of enlightenment through business: remember to show gratitude for the people who help you be successful. If you have employees, it's important to treat them well. The way you treat your employees will be reflected in how they treat your business. Happy employees make a successful company, and employees always talk about their employer: don't' give them a reason to say negative things.

We learned a lot together throughout this book, so let's take a quick look at some of the most important things you need to remember:

- You are a warrior riding a unicorn, but you have horses on the brain! You can turn your dreams

into reality with a little hard work and an eye towards personal and professional development.
- Every person has a unique personality that determines how they create and engage with the world around them. By honoring what makes you truly unique, you can create a business from what you love because you will create products that are as unique as you are.
- Finding and expressing your passion will make the world a better place because passion begets passion.
- Being in love with what you do does not mean that you will always feel like you are in love with what you do. Hard work can be frustrating, and your passion will wax and wane depending on your stress level. Learn how to cope with stress and failure to keep going when times get tough.
- Passive income doesn't mean that you don't have to work hard to earn money. It means that you are successfully using time leveraging, referral marketing, and thoughtful planning to grow a business without putting in as much direct involvement.

- When you switch from an active to a passive role is up to you and what you want for your life.
- Writing a good business plan takes time, and it is something you will learn as you go.
- Not everything has to happen overnight. Your growth should be determined by where you are, who you are, where you want to go, and who you want to become along the way.
- Becoming wealthy does not simply happen. You have to make it happen. Rich people use their money to make more money by investing in other businesses, owning more than one business, and making wise decisions regarding all of their financial endeavors.

-

Still not sure what it's all about?

I want you to keep in mind the following vital information that many do not know:

- You must learn to recognize opportunities when they appear in front of you.

- Then you must take attitude and action about them.

I am an author who is passionate about helping others to live a fulfilling life spiritually and financially. I worked on this book with one important message in mind: I want to give everyone the opportunity to build their wealth and success in life.

This book is a summary of conclusions from a very long period of my life, a dark period from a financial standpoint. I suppose that my readers passed through a difficult time or they are currently in a difficult financial time. What I want you to know is, I am yet to find my way to wisdom and financial independence. We all want it, after all. All seek to provide safety for loved ones, a safe financial future, and protection.

What I want to tell you finally is: don`t give up. It will get better over time. Patience and persistence will lead to your goals. This book is focused on the psychology needed to get where you want. If my information presented in the book will help you toward your goal, I declare myself satisfied spiritually.

I am glad if I could help at least one person going through a difficult time.

Visualizing and daydreaming are both essential to understanding what you want in life. Visualizing is based in reality, and daydreaming is based on your wildest fantasies. You should use both when your planning for your future.

Copyright © 2016 by Luke F. Gregory

www.ingramcontent.com/pod-product-compliance
Lightning Source LLC
Chambersburg PA
CBHW070317190526
45169CB00005B/1655